Endorsements

"Busy people rejoice! It doesn't have to be this way. More coffee isn't the solution, less sleep isn't the answer. Let Jeff guide you into a new way to be productive without just running from task to task with manic speed."

—Jon Acuff, New York Times bestselling author
of *Finish: Give Yourself the Gift of Done*

"When Jeff Sanders puts pen to paper he means it. *The Free-Time Formula* is a no nonsense guide to getting your best work done. If you're looking to increase focus and productivity, this is the book for you."

—Dean Karnazes, Ultramarathoner and New York Times
bestselling author of *Ultramarathon Man*

"If you want to get your most important work done but feel you "don't have time," then read this! The step-by-step action plan will walk you through the journey from busy and chaotic to productive and accomplished."

—Claire Diaz-Ortiz, award-winning author
and Silicon Valley innovator

"When so many other productivity gurus teach superficial hacks and 'effortless' solutions, Jeff Sanders pushes us to do the real (often hard!) work to create quality free time—by first deciding what truly matters, then cultivating the discipline to do only that. If you're tired of quick fixes that don't fix anything, and ready to go to work identifying and uprooting the real causes of the procrastination, friction, and stress in your life—so that you can spend it doing work that matters—then *The Free-Time Formula* is an absolute must-read."

—Matt Frazier, author of *No Meat Athlete*
and *The No Meat Athlete Cookbook*

"Time is money. Yadda yadda. We've heard it before. But realize it's the only thing in our lives we never get back. Jeff gives you concrete things to get more time back in your life to do the things you REALLY want to do."

—Noah Kagan, founder of Sumo.com and #30 employee at Facebook

"*The Free-Time Formula* is a must-read if you want to get your most important work done, but just can't find the time. The step-by-step action plan that Jeff gives you is revolutionary."

—Hal Elrod, author of *The Miracle Morning*

"This is not a repackaged restatement of the same things we've all read before about time management. *The Free-Time Formula* is a truly practical guide that is full of insights and actionable tips for getting your schedule and your to-do list under control. More than that, it's a book that will inspire and motivate the reader to *take action.* I took notes while reading it and have made plans to implement some of Jeff's smart advice in my own life. His "green pen" approach alone is worth the price of the book!"

—Laura McClellan, lawyer, writer, and host
of *The Productive Woman* podcast

"We're all 'busy,' but with the right focus you'll find productivity, and through productivity you'll find happiness. In *The Free-Time Formula,* Jeff provides the step-by-step guidance you need to IGNITE your business and life."

—John Lee Dumas, host of the *Entrepreneurs on Fire* podcast

"Ready to get more done and feel great while doing it? Grab *The Free-Time Formula.* Jeff Sanders goes above and beyond with a step-by-step process for finding more time, efficiency, and serenity every single day."

—Pamela Wilson, founder *BIG Brand System*
and author of *Master Content Marketing*

"Who better to walk us through the keys to finding more happiness, focus, and productivity than Jeff Sanders? Jeff's step-by-step framework will help anyone struggling with the busyness of life find peace while knocking their goals out of the park."

—Jeff Brown, award-winning broadcaster and host
of the *Read to Lead Podcast*

"This is the book every busy leader needs. Full of practical advice and actionable strategies, *The Free-Time Formula* is your antidote to the poison of busyness."

—Dr. Brian Dixon, founder of *Amplify Publishers*

"In *The Free-Time Formula* Jeff functions as a self-aware sherpa leading us out of overwhelm and into a new place of intentionality. Discover how peace and productivity can co-exist as your new norm."

—Kary Oberbrunner, author of *Elixir Project*
and *Day Job to Dream Job*

"Jeff is an efficiency machine. He not only studies efficiency and productivity but he lives it out. This book gives you a step-by-step action plan on how to get more done with your time."

—Grant Baldwin, keynote speaker and founder of *The Speaker Lab*

"This book is not about time management—it is about life management. You will learn how to plan the life you want so you don't live a life you don't want."

—Lee Cockerell, executive vice president, Walt Disney World
(retired) and author of *Time Management Magic*

"The best-selling author of *The 5 AM Miracle* has miraculously managed to do it again. In *The Free-Time Formula*, Jeff Sanders not only addresses our greatest fears surrounding success, but provides a compelling blueprint for the only kind of success that really matters: the meaningful kind. This book is a must-read for anyone who realizes that the only ladder of success that matters is the one leaning against the right tree!"

—August Turak, author of *Business Secrets of the Trappist Monks*

"Jeff Sanders's *The Free-Time Formula* humanizes personal productivity and shows that it's possible for everybody, even YOU, to get more from the time you have."

—David Hooper, host of *BIG Podcast*

"Imagine being able to fully apply your attention and energy where and when you need it most. Jeff Sanders walks you through why free time is the hidden secret of achieving this. Stop distractions, start eliminating nonsense from your life, and make the most of your time and energy."

—Erik Fisher, host of the *Beyond the To-Do List* podcast

"Finally, someone said it—we can be super productive, busy, and wonderfully ambitious and still create time to enjoy our hard work!"

—Andy Ramage, co-founder of OneYearNoBeer
and author of *The 28-Day Alcohol-Free Challenge*

"Jeff has already helped me rethink what I should do at 5 a.m. each day. In *The Free-Time Formula*, Jeff helps us develop the plan and gives us permission to reimagine how we spend our most limited resource—our time."

—Dave Delaney, founder of Futureforth and author
of *New Business Networking*

"Jeff uses great storytelling to help us slow down so we can speed up and get more out of our day. This is a great read for anyone who wants to escape the trap of busyness and achieve a better tomorrow."

—Scott Friesen, Busyness Killer and founder of Simpletivity

THE
FREE-TIME
FORMULA

For Nicholas

Jeff Sa

For Nicholas

THE FREE-TIME FORMULA

Finding Happiness, Focus, and Productivity No Matter How Busy You Are

JEFF SANDERS

WILEY

Published by John Wiley & Sons, Inc., Hoboken, New Jersey.

Published simultaneously in Canada.

For general information on our other products and services or for technical support, please contact our Customer Care Department within the United States at (800) 762-2974, outside the United States at (317) 572-3993 or fax (317) 572-4002.

Wiley publishes in a variety of print and electronic formats and by print-on-demand. Some material included with standard print versions of this book may not be included in e-books or in print-on-demand. If this book refers to media such as a CD or DVD that is not included in the version you purchased, you may download this material at http://booksupport.wiley.com. For more information about Wiley products, visit www.wiley.com.

Library of Congress Cataloging-in-Publication Data

Names: Sanders, Jeff, 1984- author.
Title: The free-time formula : finding happiness, focus, and productivity no
    matter how busy you are / Jeff Sanders.
Description: Hoboken, New Jersey : John Wiley & Sons, Inc., [2018] | Includes index. |
Identifiers: LCCN 2017056125 (print) | LCCN 2017057057 (ebook) | ISBN
    9781119432982 (epub) | ISBN 9781119432975 (pdf) | ISBN 9781119432968 (cloth)
Subjects: LCSH: Time management.
Classification: LCC BF637.T5 (ebook) | LCC BF637.T5 S345 2018 (print) |
    DDC 650.1/1—dc23
LC record available at https://lccn.loc.gov/2017056125

Cover Design: Wiley
Cover Image: Background: © mammuth/iStockphoto;
            Beaker: © sorn11/iStockphoto

Printed in the United States of America

10 9 8 7 6 5 4 3 2 1

For my wife, Tessa, the reason I am able to find my own happiness, focus, and productivity.

Contents

Foreword

Imagine if you could get an extra hour of free time, every single day—to read, to work out, or to spend with your family.

What if you could double your productivity while eliminating those feelings of being overworked and overwhelmed?

Seems impossible? That's what I thought too until I experienced it myself.

A long time ago I believed success was all about the hustle. Working five days a week wasn't enough so I worked seven. Eight hours a day wasn't enough so I worked sixteen or more, often sleeping just a few hours under my desk. I was "crazy busy" and wore my insane schedule like a badge of honor. "I'll sleep when I'm dead," I'd say with bravado.

And that almost happened. One early morning I stopped to fill up my car with gas and when I drove away, *klunk*! I had forgotten to take the nozzle out of my car. I was lucky I didn't blow the place up. A week later I was pulled over by a state trooper. He told me he was driving the speed limit in the slow lane when I pulled up behind him and rode his bumper, then

I swerved around him and sped off ultimately doing ninety miles per hour. *And I never saw him until his siren went off and his lights flashed in my rearview mirror.* I was so tired, stressed, and not present that I was like a drunk who just didn't understand how many drinks I had.

That breaking point led me to a long study of productivity, time management, and mindfulness. I've interviewed hundreds of ultra-productive people including self-made millionaires and billionaires, Olympic athletes, and even straight-A college students. What were their secrets to extreme productivity?

With my last company, I went from working a hundred hours a week for my little $1-million-a-year business to thirty-two hours a week in a $12-million-a-year business. Twelve times the results with one-third the work. When I sold that business, to celebrate, I bought a painting by renowned New York City artist Peter Tunney. It's called *The Time Is Always Now*.

Today, I'm devoting my life to helping others achieve their full potential. My company, LEADx, offers free online training programs to everyone around the world. We reach people in 192 different countries and universally our most popular courses are on overcoming procrastination, choosing priorities, increasing focus, and maximizing energy. The desire for more time is universal, because time is life.

That's what makes Jeff Sanders's *The Free-Time Formula* literally life-changing. He shares not just research from other leading productivity experts, but also, with total vulnerability, the mistakes he's made and lessons he's learned on his own journey to greater focus and happiness.

And be prepared to be pushed out of your comfort zone. Like a magic mirror, this book will reveal where you truly are in your own life, it will reveal your distraction habits, and other ways you self-sabotage your success. I definitely squirmed in discomfort as I answered Jeff's questions and completed the self-assessment and realized how much further I have to go. But I know you can't have an extraordinary life by doing what you've always done.

How would an extra hour or two a day change your life? How could that time make a positive impact on your health, happiness, and family? There are 1,440 minutes in a day. As each minute passes, you never get it back. Remember, the time is always now.

Kevin Kruse
New York Times best-selling author of
15 Secrets Successful People Know About Time Management and CEO of LEADx

Introduction

THE DARK SIDE OF PRODUCTIVITY

Six weeks after signing the papers to write this book about free time, happiness, and productivity, I found myself (for the first time), as a patient in the emergency room.

The doctor concluded I had suffered an esophageal spasm, a condition that closely resembles a heart attack and is presumed to be caused in part by stress and anxiety (Whelan, 2017).

How did I get here? How did a guy in his thirties, a productivity coach and marathon runner, find himself so overworked that his own body revolted against him? How did a beautifully manicured calendar with ambitious goals turn into an uncontrollable monster with such an extreme consequence?

Most importantly, how can *you* craft your own productive, fulfilling, and successful life, while ensuring a situation like this one does not happen to you?

This book is about so much more than free time. It is about so much more than an extra hour of Netflix, or another night out on the town. This book is about designing your ideal world and experiencing the extraordinary benefits that come with it.

BURSTING AT THE SEAMS

Let's back this story up just a bit. There is a lot to unfold here.

One year before my surprising medical fiasco I was in a good place. I was working hard, accomplishing goals left and right, and riding a wave of hope, optimism, and some seriously great outcomes.

Right in the middle of this productive season I got sick and took a few days off to recover. I was beaten up, exhausted, and long overdue for a break.

Though my physician told me I had caught a seasonal bug, I knew the truth: I had caused this illness. I had pushed too hard, asked for too much, and believed I was invincible (*which is pretty typical Jeff Sanders behavior*). Knowing that I tend to lean on my natural ambition (and quite a few shots of espresso), it was clear I needed a new plan to ease into my goals. I needed a new rhythm, more flex time, and a balanced approach to my entire calendar.

I tried a new approach and, surprisingly to me, it worked wonders. For a full year, I was crushing my goals while not getting crushed myself. For twelve whole months, I managed to get more done than I expected and avoid any serious lapses in productivity.

But...(*you may have seen this coming*)...it did not last. I got greedy. I became overly ambitious (*again*) and began to uncontrollably take on more than I could reasonably handle. My projects were growing bigger in scale, I was saying yes to more opportunities than I had time for, and, most importantly, I was squeezing every last ounce of margin out of my life.

Free time? Nah! I had work time.

Breaks? Nope. I was on fire, remember?

Then, one by one, the precursors to the ER began to appear. Because I had booked my schedule to the brim, there was no free space for anything else, including the inevitable problems that always show up in the process of doing anything significant.

Let's get specific.

In eight short weeks I booked and delivered back-to-back-to-back speaking engagements; recorded and edited the audiobook for *The 5 AM Miracle* (my first book); negotiated the contract for the book you are reading now; launched a premium productivity membership program; scaled up my exercise routine to six days a week; continued recording, editing, and publishing weekly episodes of my podcast—and I continued to manage any and all personal responsibilities I have with my wife, Tessa; our home; our pug, Benny; our finances; and on, and on.

You can likely see where this is headed. There was no wiggle room, no flexibility, no free time. Though I could not see it myself, I was teetering on a total breakdown, and it was only a matter of time before I would come crashing down.

Without warning, and in the final seven days of this eight-week calamity, my life went from busy and productive to chaotic and unmanageable. On top of all of the many projects I was working so hard on, three formidable and unforeseen problems fell right into my lap.

I found myself arguing over a contentious contract dispute with an important client, fighting a collections issue over a hospital billing error, and receiving challenging family medical news that only added additional debt, stress, and frustrating uncertainty.

This was a formula for disaster—a shining example of building a frail house of cards and then helplessly watching as the foundation gives way.

Each challenge was daunting on its own. As they began to stack up, one after the other, it was becoming clear that I was losing the tight grip I valued so much over the projects and opportunities I had personally accepted, and relinquishing any ability I had to respond to setbacks I never saw coming.

I was beginning to feel the substantial weight and crushing magnitude of my current commitments and brand-new obligations. Without a minute of flex time on my calendar, and my stress already rising to an all-time high, I was out of options to realistically complete the tasks at hand.

A few days later my wife called 911 when I found myself with heart attack–like symptoms: rapid heart rate, shortness of breath, rising blood pressure, nausea, and extreme tightness in my chest—essentially, a full-on panic attack that felt as though death was knocking at my front door. Thirty minutes later I was riding in an ambulance to the nearest Nashville emergency room, and confronting my poor decision making that allowed this mess to occur.

A perfect storm arose, and I was crushed beneath it.

A LIFE ON LESS

Fast-forward a few months and my life, business, and daily calendar had all transformed in dramatic ways.

No longer was I planning epic goals on top of one another, or booking fourteen-hour workdays on purpose. Instead, I found myself with an extraordinary situation that still makes me smile today. I had free time—real time to process my life and goals—time to address the unpredictable challenges that inevitably pop up—AND focused time to make significant progress on my most important work.

The irony is not lost on me—I needed "free time" to write *The Free-Time Formula,* and I made it happen.

There are many lessons to be learned from our most challenging seasons in life: consequences we should avoid, problems we should prevent, distracting people we should block on Facebook...

And I believe there is also so much to be gained from reviewing our victories, digging deep into the seasons of life when everything flows smoothly, analyzing our brightest moments, and figuring out how we can repeat those successes over and over again.

When I think back to that tough season of my life that resulted in an unexpected ER visit, I am forced to confront difficult but powerful questions—and you too can ask yourself these same questions about your current challenges and vision for the future:

1. Do you have all of the precious time you need right now to fully process the busyness of modern daily life?
2. Are your current goals serving you, or are they serving someone else's agenda, external validation, arbitrary checkboxes, or blind ambition?
3. Are you in the habit of self-sabotage, undermining your progress just when things start to go well?
4. Do you consistently respond to unexpected yet inevitable challenges with clear focus, wisdom, and patience?
5. If your current reality continues as it is going now, will you become the person you always hoped to become?

6. Do you have guaranteed blocks of time on your calendar for what matters most today, and every day going forward?
7. What transformative actions can you take now to clear the nonsense from your calendar and be at your best every day?

The answers to questions just like these are what this book is all about. There is a lot we can do to build ourselves up to handle more every day, but there is infinitely more we can do to design a life that operates beautifully on less.

The process to find more happiness, focus, and productivity lies in *The Free-Time Formula.* Carving out free time for our most valuable ambitions (*and our sanity*) in the midst of a busy life is more of an art than a science, but the productive building blocks are here, and I am excited to share them with you!

STEP

I

Find Out What's Really Going On

1

The Freedom to Do Anything

We All Want More Free Time, Right?

All of your time is free time—every minute.

That can be a hard pill to swallow, especially when we are bombarded with responsibilities, obligations, and important tasks to accomplish every week of every year. However, as you will soon see, you have an incredible opportunity with the time you already have, with the work you are already doing, and with the calendar you know is already overbooked (again).

Working on goals that matter to us is what we are here to do, and no matter how you define it, your time is your time. How you choose to spend it is influenced by more factors than we have time to unpack in this book, but let's start with the biggest chunk for most people: work.

FREE TIME: AN EXCUSE TO KEEP WORKING

I know this is the Type A in me speaking loudly, but work is not the enemy—it is one of our greatest means to fulfillment and goal achievement. Work is a love affair with our inner creative and a real opportunity to leave the world better than we found it.

My wife, Tessa, and I are self-identified workaholics, and we both work from home. We naturally fill our free time with more work because we genuinely love what we do.

Every Friday night is date night for the two of us—a chance to stop working, get out of the house, and eat dinner together somewhere in Nashville. I would love to say that we have tried all of the best restaurants, but we are way too predictable (and cheap) for that. If not tacos at Las Palmas, then tacos at Taco Mamacita. If not Mamacita's, then back to Las Palmas. Tacos win almost every week.

Date night used to be scheduled at 5:00 pm, then 5:30, then 6:00. A few weeks ago, we skipped it because both of us would rather finish our projects than leave anything undone. Though Tessa and I intentionally schedule free time on our calendar to be filled with a night out, we ultimately choose in the moment how we want that time to be spent.

Free time becomes a placeholder on our calendar for priority management fighting against impulsivity. In other words, in the open spaces on our calendar we could tackle our responsibilities and goals, or spontaneously do whatever we want. Knowing the two of us, "whatever we want" often means choosing to extend our workday a little longer.

This choice comes with its own set of pros and cons, but when you genuinely love what you do, working a few extra hours can often bring more satisfaction than clocking out early to get a jump start on the weekend. On the flip side, you could find yourself working to the bone and falling into the trap of staying busy because it is the only thing you know how to do.

FREE TIME: THE ULTIMATE ESCAPE

Free time can also be your greatest chance to do anything other than what you dislike. We often plan to leave open blocks of time on our calendars (mostly nights and weekends) so that we can stop doing whatever it is we have been doing all week. In other words, we hate our jobs and are dying to do absolutely anything else.

Given the opportunity to do *absolutely anything* in an open block of time, we do a little dance because it sounds so intriguing and hopeful. Here, the term *free time* is seductive. It infers that we never have enough of it and that something amazing will happen when it shows up.

It is easy to dream about how time away from the office could be spent surfing the ocean, climbing mountains, or rereading *Fifty Shades of Grey*, but what do you do in the moment?

How is your current free time being occupied? Is it routinely as fulfilling and rejuvenating as you hoped?

Chances are that you actually have enormously more free time than you realize, but you just call it something different:

• Me time
• Family time
• Boys' night out
• Girls' night in
• Napping
• Hustling

- Training
- Catching up on *Game of Thrones*

Wanting more free time to unwind and relax is admirable and necessary to balance out the stress of life, assuming you define *free time* as any time outside the office . . . or the kids . . . or the spouse . . . or the dog . . . or the _____ (you get the picture).

Defining what free time means to you is the most important first step to ensuring you get as much of it as you want.

THE MYTH OF FREE TIME

The thing about free time is that it is up to you to define what it means, how you use it, and how much of it you believe is necessary to achieve a healthy sense of balance (*which is a word that is often misused and results in lots of guilt*).

Free time is a myth. It has never existed and it never will.

Every minute of every day is up to you. There are no restrictions. You can do whatever you want, whenever you want.

As radical as that sounds, it is true.

You can get up off your couch and go for a run right now. You can walk into your boss's office and quit right now.

If you choose, you can change the entire course of your life in an instant—this instant.

Now, most of us would never take advantage of this fact because we box ourselves in with occupations, families, mortgages, and other self-created boundaries to define and optimize our time here on earth (and to avoid winding up homeless, alone, or in jail).

And this is a good thing.

I am not arguing that because we all have the freedom to do anything that we should. Quite the opposite—because we can do anything, we have to choose very carefully how our time is spent, or the whole thing falls apart.

Having the power to choose what to do with every waking minute is an enormous responsibility that most of us surrender to societal structures, employers, family members, or the latest hit series on YouTube. *(I will not quote Spiderman right now, but you know that line is coming next, don't you?)*

And yet, it is true, you do have incredible power to choose how you spend your time, and you do have the responsibility to make the most of it.

THE TIME MANAGEMENT CONUNDRUM

Time management is a bit of a farce. You can never actually manage time because it moves forward at its own pace, regardless of what we do.

Activities, on the other hand, are up to us.

We get to choose what to engage in or disengage from. We get to opt in or opt out, say yes or say no, get roped into something, or wiggle our way out of it.

The greatest challenge with managing our many activities is doing so inside the time box of twenty-four hours. Though time is technically infinite, daylight is not. We are only awake for so long before we crash and pass out.

This clear daily boundary leaves us with a problem most of us (including myself) struggle to overcome. There is just too much to do in the few hours we have each day—too many responsibilities, too many obligations, too many *everythings* that seem to never end.

The abundance of choice is paralyzing, overwhelming, and exhausting. More opportunities exist today than ever, which means more work exists today than ever. We are stressed out because life is inherently stressful. The challenge is ubiquitous and, without a clear plan, very few among us can escape the trap of this modern mayhem.

In my work as a productivity coach, I see a few common problems that appear to affect nearly everyone, and most on a daily basis.

Too much, too often

Having more work to accomplish in shorter time spans may be the most prolific problem in most companies and households, and on most personal calendars.

Downsizing causes those left over to take on more tasks, family members find themselves solving problems for others instead of addressing their own responsibilities, and the twenty-four-hour clock never gets any bigger.

The problem is not that more work actually needs to get done, it is that more nonsense needs to get cut. A clear lack of priorities leads to the chaos, overwhelm, and stress that accumulates from doing too much, too often.

Working harder only gets you so far. Working faster can only last for so long. Working on nonessentials wastes even more precious time, and saying yes to yet another task adds to the already overinflated schedule.

Last-minute catastrophes

I frequently survey the subscribers to my email newsletter about their productivity mistakes and pitfalls.

One question asks, "*What is your biggest frustration around your own productivity?*" The most common answer is **procrastination**—waiting until the last minute and avoiding the work that needs to get done right up until it's almost too late.

The last-minute stress that builds up as a deadline nears can be debilitating. Yes, some people thrive on pressure, but not many do so well when that pressure never lets up. When we find ourselves prioritizing activities that never had to get done in the first place, we find ourselves panicking as the clear priorities float to the top of the list just as they need to be addressed.

More coffee! now!

If a pot of coffee could solve all of our productivity problems, you and I both would likely just hook up an IV drip of dark roast espresso and start bulldozing through our bucket lists.

The challenge with productivity in this sense revolves around naturally derived energy and focus—two elements that, when combined, create a powerhouse of potential.

Most office environments serve up endless opportunities for staying awake to burn the candle at both ends without ever truly crafting a solution to stay alert and centered on one thing at a time.

Longer work hours, collaborative office environments, increased demands, and a heavy reliance on stimulants just to get through the day also introduce a slew of health problems from poor sleep and weight gain to high blood pressure and eventual trips to a marriage counselor.

It is not a pretty picture.

When results are prioritized above sustainability, when productivity is prioritized above sanity, and when "trying to get it all done" is prioritized above *doing only what matters*, we find ourselves trapped in a prison of perfectionism.

When the bar is too high, it is too high, and there comes a point when the madness has to stop.

A DANGEROUS WORD

I wrote this book for one specific and clear reason: *productivity is a dangerous word*.

The double-edged sword of getting more done is that you can check more boxes, and so you do—over and over again. Doing more is alluring and certainly provides clear benefits, but (as we just discussed) at enormous costs.

The opposite is also true.

When I tell people I teach others how to get more done, it is quite common to see a reaction of *"Oh, I don't need MORE to do...."* In other words, we know we are doing too much already, and the last thing we want is to have to do more in order to do less.

No one actually needs another book on getting things done, or another ten-step online video course on achieving four-hour workweeks, and yet we struggle day in and day out with balance. We *still* never can get it all done.

FREE TIME AT ITS FINEST

We are having the wrong conversation about productivity. We should be talking about how to do less when all we ever do is talk about how to do more. What is really going on here?

This is not an anti-productivity book, but it was designed to help you outsmart the temptation and repercussion of doing more in order to optimize the few things that actually provide the outcomes you have been striving so hard to produce.

Saying you should work smarter, not harder is a bit cliché, but if it works for you, own it. Work as intelligently as you can.

This book is here to help you make critical changes to your calendar, outwit your nemesis of distraction, and redesign your life with more clarity and resolve than ever before.

Free time at its finest is when your calendar serves you, and not itself or someone else. When open blocks of time show up again and again, you have a tremendous opportunity to live differently, to change the lives of those around you, and to secure a more prosperous future.

If you would like more freedom to pursue your grandest goals, or even just enough downtime to take a solid nap, you are in the right place. With more free time comes more creative breakthroughs, clarity on your most important goals, and the freedom to choose how to live your best life.

The steps to reach this new life are about to unfold.

THE FREE-TIME FORMULA

The Free-Time Formula is a seven-step system to help you find happiness, focus, and productivity no matter how busy you are.

It is a path to high achievement without the burden of slaving away 24/7 to get there. In short, it is a process to cut the nonsense, focus, and achieve more than ever.

The seven steps

This book is divided into seven steps (or parts), aligned to the seven steps of the formula, with two chapters dedicated to each step:

1. Find Out What's Really Going On
2. Clarify What Matters
3. Flex Your Muscles
4. Cut the Nonsense
5. Schedule What Matters
6. Prevent Future Nonsense
7. Solidify Your Ideal Rhythm

The process is designed to be sequential, as each step builds upon the lessons from the previous steps.

You can feel free to work through each component one at a time at your own pace. There is no required time element for any step, though I do provide a seven-day action plan at the end to help jump-start your progress.

Also, to expedite the process for you to get results, skip chapters. As a productivity strategy, it is wise to never read any book word for word unless the information is incredibly dense and epically important for your future.

Read what you need now, take action, and then come back at a future date for the other content.

Guaranteeing more free time on your calendar can be as simple as cutting a current event from your calendar, or as complex as restructuring your entire life from the ground up.

The Free-Time Formula provides the flexibility to take either approach. Whether you are just looking for a few quick wins, or a new start at life, the formula will help you break down the steps and make it happen.

Here is a quick rundown of each step in the formula:

Step I: Find Out What's Really Going On
The first step in *The Free-Time Formula* is designed to bring self-awareness front and center. You will conduct a

self-evaluation and time audit to determine how each day plays out for you. This information will determine just how much progress is possible.

Step II: Clarify What Matters
The second step will highlight the vital few priorities that truly mean something in your life now. We will examine warning signs to see if you are off track from your goals and filter your ideas to gain clarity on what to do next.

Step III: Flex Your Muscles
There are few things, if any, that I value more than my own health. One of the most powerful forces that will allow you to do your best work every day is being in the best physical and mental shape of your life. In the third step, we will focus on quick yet highly effective strategies for boosting your energy, physical fitness, and mental acuity.

Step IV: Cut the Nonsense
In the fourth step, you will have the chance to purge. There is always more going on than is necessary, and you will begin to build the efficient systems that will reduce friction and get you to point B faster.

Step V: Schedule What Matters
In step five you will have the opportunity to fill all of that wonderful new free time on your calendar with meaningful goals. I will also break down how to craft your own Red-Carpet Calendar and how to effectively schedule what matters most every week.

Step VI: Prevent Future Nonsense
In the sixth step, we will fight against our greatest nemesis, distraction. I will provide strategies to help you block yourself and others when it matters most.

Step VII: Solidify Your Ideal Rhythm

Finally, in the seventh step, we will establish your daily rhythm of digging hard into your work and then take a big step back to strategize more intelligently. This final component wraps up the formula with a clear seven-day action plan.

Free Bonuses

Readers of *The Free-Time Formula* get free access to a variety of bonus materials to supplement the book including a guided workbook, book club questions, templates, and more. Sign up: www.JeffSanders.com/FreeTimeBonus.

GRAB YOUR (DIGITAL) HIGHLIGHTER

As with everything I create, this book is designed with a single purpose in mind: *to get results for you through direct action.*

Action is the key differentiator between an idea and a medal around your neck. I have conversations nearly every week with well-meaning and highly educated folks who believe they have read everything about productivity, and yet find themselves struggling.

Get your highlighter ready; this is quotable:

Knowledge is a means to an end, NOT the result itself.

Read that sentence again. It is true. I know it sounds crazy, especially if you are in academia, but this will save you a ton of time.

Productivity is an action game—not a contest against your neighbors to see who can get the most Amazon Prime drones delivering stacks of books to your front door. Dusty books on a shelf will not make you run a marathon, start a business, or build your dream home in the foothills of the Appalachian Mountains.

Knowing dozens of productivity strategies is vastly different from *consistently applying* them AND *getting tremendous results* because of them.

Highlight that one too.

I once skimmed through the popular personal development book *The Slight Edge* by Jeff Olson. I was underwhelmed, so I put the book down and ignored it.

One day I was reminded of the advice I am giving you right now. I went back to the book, looked at it a little closer, and had to catch my breath.

Yes, I knew many of the lessons, stories, and strategies in the book because I had read so many other personal growth books in the past, but (and this is the key to everything), I was not actually *doing* many of the strategies. *Ah!*

Talk about a wake-up call. This smack in the face was all I needed to get up, move, and start changing my life.

Knowing something is never the same as doing it—ever.

Also, despite my paperless lifestyle, I am obsessed with physical books and audiobooks. I have never read a single digital book from cover to cover, and I do not plan to anytime soon.

For the sake of this book, you can choose any medium that gets you from point A to point B—but you have to get there.

Point B is at the *end* of this book, and there are dozens of new ideas, strategies, and action steps waiting for you to discover.

So, let's get to it!

QUICK REVIEW: *FREEDOM TO DO ANYTHING*

1. **Free time is a myth.**
   Every minute of every day is up to you; however, because time is limited and you can do anything with it, you have

to choose very carefully which activities rise to the top and warrant precious space on your calendar.

2. **There is just too much to do.**
There is almost always too much scheduled in the few hours we have each day—too many responsibilities, too many obligations, too many *everythings* that seem to never end. To face the challenges of modern daily life, we need a clear plan to focus on the few things that matter most.

3. **Your ticket to freedom lies in *The Free-Time Formula.***
With the seven-step system in this book, you can cut the nonsense in your life to focus and achieve more than ever.

CHAPTER 1 ACTION PLAN

1. Stop.
Before you move on to chapter 2, I would like to guarantee that the promise I am making to you with this book is fulfilled. To do that, we need to get you a tangible result right now.

Yes, now is the time to stop reading and do something in this moment. This is not homework; it is *self*-work—the whole point of this book. Pick something, anything that will tangibly make tomorrow easier, smoother, or more productive. I recommend being a little bold and doing something dramatic.

Small, consistent changes are the most effective over the long-term, but big action makes you feel good now. Go big.

Then, email me and tell me about it, jeff@jeffsanders.com. I respond to every email within twenty-four hours, so let's build this relationship right away. I do not want you going through this book on your own.

Radical change is often too complicated to attempt by yourself, plus you get to chat with the author. I know that means something because I frequently interview many of my favorite authors on my podcast. Talking to them greatly enhances my reading experience, and dramatically increases the odds that I will take direct action with the book's content.

(Cheat: If you would like, you can use Step #2 below as your action. It is a good one!)

2. **Start a daily journal.**

Find a place to take notes about the inconsistencies you find as you move throughout your day.

Just like when you buy a red car, and all of a sudden you see dozens of red cars you never knew were there before, when you begin thinking about efficiency and productivity you will see opportunities around every corner to improve your systems, cut excess noise, and get more done.

3. **Grab your (digital) highlighter.**

It's time to jump right in!

2

Asking the Right Questions

Which Disney Princess Are You?

In one of my absent-minded moments I stumbled upon a BuzzFeed quiz titled, "Which Disney Princess Are You?"

Was I tempted?

Yes.

Did I stop doing my most important work and fall victim to this silly online distraction?

You bet!

Turns out I am Cinderella: *"Hardworking and industrious, you are the ideal co-worker. You burn the midnight oil to get projects done and often pick up the slack for others. Most likely you were valedictorian of your class"* (BuzzFeed, 2017).

Honestly, that just about sums it up, except the part about being an ideal coworker (I work for myself for a reason).

Online quizzes like these are akin to the most addictive drug you can imagine. We are hardwired for validation. We are egomaniacs, and we are at the mercy of anyone who understands basic human psychology.

Marketers use these tactics to capture our attention by appealing to our most shallow desires. This works well for advertising, but it also paints a clear picture of us.

Beyond wanting to simply avoid our work for a few minutes and engage in a trivial digital diversion, we actually want to know more about ourselves. We want to be sure we are on the right path, that we understand our role in the world, and that we can use this knowledge to improve our lives in countless ways.

Knowing that I am a quantifiable Cinderella does not tell me anything I did not already know about myself, but it does validate my vision of who I want to be.

With that kind of knowledge and affirmation from a third party (including personality tests like the DiSC Profile or Myers-Briggs Type Indicator), I can convert the description of my personality and preferences into a workable plan of action.

For example, if I know that Cinderella is "hardworking and industrious," I can choose to embody those characteristics and start proving that sentiment to be true.

So, what kind of achiever are you?

Are you hardworking and industrious like Cinderella, outgoing and vivacious like Mulan, or daring and adventurous like Jasmine?

I am not asking you to stop reading the book and take this specific quiz . . . but if you must, I will wait.

STEP I: FIND OUT WHAT'S REALLY GOING ON

The first step of *The Free-Time Formula* is to channel your inner Disney Princess—or, phrased another way, to analyze your present reality and discover exactly who you are today in this season of your life.

In the first chapter, we examined the myth of free time and looked at the current reality of many hardworking and overly busy professionals. Now we will clarify where you are today and explore how your circumstances are affecting you.

The power of self-awareness

Knowing more about your present reality and how you operate best is vital to understanding how you can optimize your life and move forward with real confidence and results.

Despite our similarities, you and I are different people with different goals in life.

My wife, Tessa, and I are incredibly similar Type A personalities with a nearly identical childhood (same hometown, same group of friends, same poster of Britney Spears hanging on the wall in our room), and yet we approach each situation with our own unique flair and creativity.

No two people are the same, and no one solution serves all of us equally.

The Free-time Formula begins with a Self-Evaluation and Time Audit, two tools that are designed to clarify your life right now—communicating how effectively you use the precious time you have available each day.

Me 101

As is common in coaching, consulting, therapy, or other prescriptive professions, the "expert" typically provides a perspective on what you *should* do.

I approach this process from another vantage point.

The self-evaluation is open-ended with considerable flexibility for you to fill in the gaps on your own. In other words, no one is here to judge you or provide a verifiable solution to your next best move.

You get to make those calls. You get to decide what your life looks like and where it should end up.

The beauty of knowing more about yourself is the power it provides you to make better decisions every day.

I argued in the first chapter that knowledge without action is useless, and nothing proves that point more than highly educated people making foolish choices because they never stopped to learn a thing about themselves.

Welcome to "Me 101," the art and science of knowing yourself inside and out.

QUICK WIN

Before I introduce the self-evaluation and the rest of *The Free-Time Formula*, here is a quick win to get you started with some additional free time: **make the most of the time you already have.**

Chances are that you have free time on your calendar this week—free time that you are secretly saving to binge on your current favorite TV series. That free time is up for grabs and you can do something with it now.

You may not have clarified your most important goals yet (we will get to that in chapter 3), but you likely know of half a dozen tasks, projects, or mini-goals that outshine couch-potato time.

The key to this quick win is to take advantage of that time now with anything that builds momentum and gets you moving toward a worthy ideal. A series of quick wins is a sure-fire method to a series of big successes down the road.

When you optimize small bits of free time today, you are jump-starting your drive to continue that process. In other words, you are redefining how you use your "down time" and beginning to make each hour more valuable.

The mindset that accompanies this type of action is the exact mindset that leads to optimizing your entire day, week, month, and year. It is the mindset that leads to high achievement, and it starts with tiny victories right now.

By the way, I wrote this *Quick Win* section of the book in one of my own random blocks of free time. No joke.

I saw the phrase "quick win" in my notes and thought, "I can do that right now!" It is that exact line of thinking that leads to tangible progress, and it works every time.

SELF-EVALUATION

This self-evaluation is a thorough analysis of where you stand today, right now, in terms of your productivity, stress, and ability to carve out time for what matters most.

Think of this as a snapshot in time, covering seven core areas of your life and work with five clarifying questions per area. My goal with this evaluation is that you will be able to do three things:

1. Quickly identify and acknowledge areas where you are excelling, along with any strategies that are pushing you directly toward your current goals.
2. Discover (or be reminded of) areas of improvement that have the power to revolutionize your daily workflow.
3. Choose one area that you believe would add the most value to your life today if it was improved immediately.

A few instructions

- Visit JeffSanders.com/FreeTimeBonus to download the Self-Evaluation and Time Audit documents (print and digital versions are available) as well as other bonuses for the book.
- Block off some time so you can fully answer each question.
- Answer based on the present day, or what is typical for you in this season.

The free-time formula self-evaluation

Physical Health

1. **Overall Health:** In a general sense, how healthy do you feel today, and most days?
2. **Nutrition:** Describe your typical diet. Do you consistently consume food and drinks that nourish your body and energize you for more work?
3. **Fitness:** Describe your current level of fitness. Do you consistently move and strengthen your body?
4. **Stress:** What role does stress play in your day-to-day life? What are your most common sources of unhealthy stress?
5. **Mental Clarity:** To the best of your ability, describe the current state of your brain, or how you think. Do you feel cloudy or clear-headed?

Energy

1. **Productive Potential:** What is working well to help you stay alert and moving forward each day?
2. **Cycles:** Do you plan your most challenging work around your daily energy cycles? How do you respond when your energy dips?

3. **Rest:** Do you regularly plan time for rest and recovery, away from your work?
4. **Stillness:** Do you make time for meditation, prayer, stillness, or another form of quiet time each day?
5. **Laughter:** Do you intentionally schedule time just for fun and games?

Relationships

1. **Family:** Are you encouraged and empowered by those you live with to pursue your goals?
2. **Partner:** What role does your spouse or partner play in your dreams? Describe your relationship and how it helps or hinders your progress.
3. **Children:** Describe your life today with your kids (or other close relatives). How do you approach balancing your goals with those of your children?
4. **Colleagues:** Describe those with whom you work closely. Do those relationships energize you or serve as an obstacle?
5. **Internet Folks:** How much time do you spend in dialogue with those you have never met in person? Is your time online well spent?

Career and Business

1. **Passion:** Do you feel empowered and energized by your work? What parts of your work light you up, and which bring you down?
2. **Trajectory:** How do you feel about your current career path? Describe how your work today serves your grander vision for the future.
3. **Lifestyle:** Does your current working schedule fit the way you want to live? Describe an ideal working day.

4. **Side Hustle:** Describe the work you do when you are off the clock. What passion projects are driving you on nights and weekends?
5. **Workload:** How much do you work now? Does your current level of work align to the balance you seek?

Finances

1. **Cash Flow:** How healthy is your bank account? Are you bringing in enough to cover expenses?
2. **Debt:** Are you proactively managing your liabilities?
3. **Fear:** What role does money play in regards to your stress? Do you frequently worry about your finances, or is there a solid plan in place?
4. **Income:** Describe your current income level. Are you where you want to be?
5. **Time:** How much of your time is traded for money? Does that align with your vision of an ideal workweek?

Productivity

1. **Game Plan:** Describe how you plan each day. Do you approach the upcoming day with a written plan? Do you schedule an appropriate number of tasks each day?
2. **Boundaries:** Do you have guaranteed focused blocks of time on your calendar for what matters most each day?
3. **Free Time:** Based on how you define free time, how much free time do you have on your calendar this week? What do you typically do during your free time?
4. **Distractions:** Do you consistently deny requests from others? How do you get back on track when you find yourself off course?
5. **Fire Drills:** What happens when something dire pops up? Do you usually have time to process the busyness of modern daily life?

Grand Goals

1. **Present Day:** Describe your current goals. Do you make consistent progress on them?
2. **Alignment:** Are your current goals serving you, or are they serving someone else's agenda, external validation, arbitrary checkboxes, or blind ambition?
3. **Big Picture:** Describe your grand life goals. What about those goals resonates with you? Describe the emotion behind your ambitious pursuits.
4. **Procrastination:** How behind are you? How much of your time is spent thinking about your goals versus making tangible progress on them?
5. **Direction:** If your current reality continues as it is going now, will you become the person you always hoped to become?

TIME AUDIT: PHASE I

You need a stalker.

Well, maybe not an actual stalker, but someone to follow you around and monitor your every move. Think of this person more like a fly on the wall, or a personal assistant whose job it is to objectively record what you are up to.

Years ago, I read a book by John Maxwell, an author and leadership coach, who asked how I would respond if he followed me around for twenty-four hours to determine where my time was being spent.

John hypothesized that he would easily be able to tell what my highest priorities were based upon my daily activities and how much time I spent with each one.

Though I do not have actual data to support John's hypothesis, you will with your very own time audit.

For this audit, our goal is to determine where your time goes in this current season, specifically, over the course of a single day. At this point, we will not focus on the past or the future, just the here and now.

The free-time formula time audit, phase I

Objectively, how is your time being spent? The first phase of the Time Audit consists of three steps. Complete each of these steps before moving on to the next chapter.

1. **Choose a Recording Device.**

   During my four years in college, I used a detailed calendaring system to record not only everything I was about to do, but also everything I had just done. I would update my calendar every day, filling in every hour of the day I was awake with a quick description of my activities.

   My calendar became a thorough record-keeping system with unbelievably helpful information. For example, I could easily see how much time I spent at social events versus the library. If my grades were slipping, the next move was obvious and verifiable.

   You can choose a method like this one, or one that makes it easy for you to record any relevant data. The key is to choose a recording device you will have access to all day. Your phone or a small notebook will do the trick.

2. **Choose the Day.**

   The day you audit your activities will ideally be a day you want to dramatically improve. If Mondays are the busiest day of your week, as mine tend to be, that could be a great choice.

When you analyze your busiest (or worst) day of the week, you are giving yourself the most valuable information about how you can make tangible progress in the future.

3. Complete the Audit.

When the big day arrives, begin recording your activities on an hourly basis. Take no more than five minutes per hour to record what you did in the previous sixty minutes.

The goal is to record information you believe to be objective, accurate, and relevant to your goal of discovering exactly how you spend your time, without fudging the data to make yourself feel better.

Most importantly, be sure to record any and all time-wasting activities, on top of the more clearly defined goal-achieving tasks.

As an example, you could record activities such as:

- Eating and meal prep
- Commuting
- Working
- Surfing the Internet
- Watching TV or online videos
- Sleeping
- Surfing the Internet (did I already mention that?)
- Etc.

In the next chapter, we will analyze the data you collected from your Self-Evaluation and Time Audit.

You will also complete Phase II of the Time Audit, which is designed to specifically quantify how much time is being spent on the goals you claim are the most important.

Q&A

1. **Do I have to evaluate my life and time usage with so much detail? Can't I just set some new goals and get started?**

   This question is undoubtedly the most common one I hear when I ask my coaching clients to reflect on their current situation before embarking on a new adventure.

   There is a lot of resistance here, and I get it.

   I am an impatient and ambitious guy myself, so I know what it is like to want to jump in the deep end without considering whether I can swim.

   Simply put: thorough evaluations provide incredibly useful information that I would not want you to miss.

   Take a minute, pause, and figure out exactly where you are, before getting lost in the weeds again.

2. **Is it going to be possible for *me* to free up any significant time on my busy calendar? What can I do if I have kids at home, a full-time job, and not a minute to spare already?**

   I hear you. I do. The answer is yes. It is possible for *you* to free up significant time, no matter how busy you are (*there is a reason that phrase is in the title of the book*).

   Simply put: the busier you are, the harder the decisions will be on what to cut. Fortunately, there is a lot we can do here, and I will be covering many different strategies on how to manage these tough choices as the book progresses. Hang with me. This is going to be fun!

3. **I am on board with wanting more free time, but do I have to have *ambitious* goals, or can I just pursue something a little less intense?**

   Ambition is subjective, so feel free to define your goals in whatever way makes the most sense to you. As a self-defined productivity junkie who loves to run marathons in the woods, I use the word "ambitious" a lot. It resonates with me, but this book is about you.

In the next chapter, we will break down the priorities that matter most in your life, no matter where they fall on someone else's spectrum of ambition.

QUICK REVIEW: *ASKING THE RIGHT QUESTIONS*

1. **Where are you?**
   The first step of *The Free-Time Formula* is to analyze your life in this season to discover more about who and where you are right now.

2. **How do you operate best?**
   Knowing more about your present reality and how you operate best is vital to understanding how you can optimize your life and move forward with real confidence and results.

3. **How do you actually spend your time?**
   Detailed self-evaluations and time audits provide valuable and useful data. Instead of moving on too quickly to your next step, take a minute, pause, and figure out exactly what is going on today before getting lost in the weeds again.

CHAPTER 2 ACTION PLAN

1. **Get a quick win.**
   Making the most of the time you already have is a great strategy to get a jump start on your progress right away. Take advantage of the open blocks that are on your calendar this week. Do something you normally would not do, to get results you normally would not get.

2. Complete the Free-Time Formula Self-Evaluation.

The evaluation is the foundation for your self-awareness and provides a starting block to build from. As the rest of the formula is presented, you will use the results from the evaluation to determine your best plan of action.

3. Complete the Free-Time Formula Time Audit.

The audit provides a clear snapshot of exactly what you spend your time doing. When you know how your time is being spent you have the best opportunity to cut significant time wasters and swiftly improve the progress on your most important goals.

Visit JeffSanders.com/FreeTimeBonus to download the Self-Evaluation and Time Audit documents, as well as other bonuses for the book.

STEP

II

Clarify What Matters

3

The Vital Few

How Many #1s Are on Your To-Do List?

On most days my task manager displays anywhere from five to twenty-five different tasks that I have scheduled for myself. For years I thought of these tasks as a list of priorities, but a few years ago I threw out that term.

My guess is that you have a dozen or more individual tasks to complete on most days. But how many of them are must-dos?

How many absolutely have to get done today?

Most importantly, how many of those tasks would you qualify as priorities?

PRIORITIES DO NOT EXIST

In Greg McKeown's *Essentialism: The Disciplined Pursuit of Less,* he points out that our use of the word "priorities" is a modern invention and it does not make any sense. "*The word priority came into the English language in the 1400s. It was singular. It meant the very first or prior thing. It stayed singular for the next five hundred years. Only in the 1900s did we pluralize the term and start talking about priorities"* (McKeown 2014, 16).

In other words, we have misconstrued and abused a simple word. We think we have two, three, or twelve priorities at any given time when in actuality we only have one because we can never have anything else.

Our misuse of the word priority is backfiring on us and causing a wave of overwhelm in our already busy lives.

Your "priorities" are making you less productive

Having more than one priority is a lie. Every time you use the plural form of that word you are lying to yourself about what matters in the present moment.

We can truly only ever do one thing at a time, and in any given moment we only have one task that is at the top of the list. We may have many tasks we would like to accomplish over the course of the next twenty-four hours, but only one task is the supreme task right now.

When you view your to-do list as a collection of priorities you are trying to live in two worlds at the same time: the present moment with one important task and a future moment with another.

Because our brain can only consciously do one thing at a time, we end up switching back and forth between ideas. This is the plight of multitasking and why it makes sense to use focused blocks of time (distraction-free time with a singular purpose) to ever do anything important.

Living in two worlds is exhausting, overwhelming, and only makes us more stressed out. What happens when you imagine a huge project, a long task list, or an overstuffed calendar?

This may be your reality every day, and if so, it is mayhem!

It is undeniably overwhelming to imagine doing a hundred things at the same time, let alone deciding which one to do first.

Five questions to assess your task list for today

Go ahead and get out your to-do list for today. Look at it closely and ask yourself these five key questions:

1. Are there any tasks on the list that I already know could be eliminated forever?
2. Are there any tasks on this list that I already know could be rescheduled for another day?
3. How many of these tasks are due today and could not be rescheduled without a phenomenal effort on my part?
4. Are there any tasks on this list that could be quickly and reasonably delegated to someone else?
5. If I had to pick just ONE task on this list to accomplish today, which one would it be?

What amazes me is that when I analyze my task list using these five questions, I always find many ways to simplify the chaos.

I always end up deleting unnecessary tasks, rescheduling projects for another day, and clearing up a lot of needed margin so that I can maintain my sanity and sense of presence throughout the day.

What you will find right away is that when you can focus on just one task, the next most important one, you can enter the zone, the magical place where nothing else matters except what is right in front of you.

Even today, as I am writing this chapter, I already know there are other important tasks to be accomplished, and none of them are my priorities. Writing this chapter is my priority at this very moment as I type these words.

My upcoming projects will wait. They will wait until it is their turn. They will wait until they become my priority, my next most urgent and important task.

It is true. Other tasks can and will wait their turn because there is no other option.

Finding peace with that reality is the one thing that will lead to lower blood pressure and greater productivity every day.

That is also why the subtitle to David Allen's famous book *Getting Things Done* is "*The Art of Stress-Free Productivity.*"

That is the goal, and it is certainly possible to achieve with a singular focus.

STEP II: CLARIFY WHAT MATTERS

Now that you have completed your self-evaluation and time audit, you likely have much more clarity about what is going on in your life at the moment.

The second step of *The Free-Time Formula* is to clarify what matters most in this season of your life, and it is divided into two parts: defining your vital few goals and determining what to do next.

What matters now will certainly change, shift, and evolve as you do, so the steps in these next two chapters will need to be repeated over time.

Define Your Vital Few Goals

1. Define your values.
2. Set your vision and update your bucket list.
3. Review your current responsibilities, obligations, and must-do projects.
4. Grab a green pen and highlight where you are excelling.
5. Analyze your Self-Evaluation and Time Audit results.
6. Commit to your vital few goals for this season.
7. Double-check your progress with Phase II of the Time Audit.

Determine What to Do Next

1. Prioritize your projects.
2. Filter your ideas.
3. Optimize pressure to your advantage.

1. DEFINE YOUR VALUES

Set aside everything for just a moment.

Clarifying your highest objectives in life is ideally based upon your highest standards for what a great life should be. Assuming you could start your life over again with a fresh new beginning, there are likely many changes, both big and small, that you would make.

Let's take a look at a classic example, knowing what you know now, what changes would you make if you could go back in time and try again?

Your values, what you consider to be of great importance, are the most important filters you use to see the world, and could dramatically shift the life-altering decisions that you have made over the years.

What you determine to be worthy and true dictates your career decisions, political persuasions, relationships, and work ethic. Having full awareness of your values, and acting on them, can change your entire life for the better.

For our purposes regarding free time:

- What values do you hold dear that are directly influencing your typical weekly schedule? (e.g., your current job or business, children or other close relationships, workout routine, etc.)
- How much do you value your health, especially in regards to the amount of time, money, and energy you commit to improving your well-being?
- How much do you value the security (or lack thereof) of your current career, especially when compared to the amount of flexibility or off-the-clock time it provides for your other goals?

2. SET YOUR VISION

I used to obsess over my bucket list.

Back in my early twenties, I would spend hours brainstorming enormous goals, thinking about all of the many adventures I could embark upon and the many places I could travel.

Today, I no longer find bucket lists valuable for practical goal achievement.

Yes, it is fun to brainstorm just how many mountains I could see myself climbing one day, but I quickly concluded that the bucket list goals were either distant fantasies with no basis in reality, or they were someone else's dream for a life I never wanted.

I no longer have a traditional bucket list to set quarterly goals, but I do use and love the exercise of brainstorming ambitious pursuits to clarify my vision of a beautiful life.

Dreaming about how your life could be on a grand scale is indicative of what you value and what your current goals would look like if they evolved significantly over time.

To craft more free time in your life today, consider these questions:

- What is the end goal of everything you are pursuing? What does it all add up to?
- If your current job or business expanded beyond your wildest dreams, is that what you want? If so, what bold actions could you take right now to jump-start that process? If not, are you in the right career?
- What ambitious personal goals have you been postponing that could radically change your life if you could make them happen now?

3. REVIEW YOUR RESPONSIBILITIES

I love doing chores.

My mother will be proud of this one, mostly because I am fairly certain she is the reason this is true about my life.

Doing the laundry, washing dishes, taking out the trash, and even paying bills are all activities I find rewarding.

As a Type A guy who finds checklists appealing, anything that allows me to accomplish a task, cross it off my list, and visually see the result brings a smile to my face and a true sense of accomplishment and fulfillment.

However, not all responsibilities fall into this personality quirk.

To fully understand what matters most to you, there needs to be a clear sense of what could go wrong if some things never got done—regardless of whether you enjoy the task or not.

If you never took out the trash, there are real consequences to that decision.

If you stopped going to work, quit mowing your grass, or gave up on shaving any body hair ever again—things are going to be real hairy real fast.

We all have responsibilities, obligations, job descriptions, and must-do projects. Though I argued that free time is a myth and that all of our time is up to us, there are clear high-value tasks that need to be completed to both prevent disasters and propel us forward.

- What clear responsibilities are on your plate today?
- What tasks or projects would cause severe problems if they never got done?
- What tasks appear to be obligations, but are in fact optional and can be removed from your task list?

4. GRAB A GREEN PEN

Green is the new red.

Green pens are the answer to many productivity problems as they do the opposite of the red ones.

While red pens are traditionally used to highlight mistakes, corrections, edits, and problem spots, green pens highlight our triumphs. They shower us with compliments and expose the amazing talents we possess.

Green pens scour through the mess of our lives and reveal the best parts: our successes, victories, and most brilliant moments.

While editing a previous book a few years ago, I noticed one big issue that kept popping up: I hated most of what I wrote. I could not stand the babble, the endless stories that went nowhere, the random advice that did not relate to my thesis, the fact that I did not have a thesis...

In a fit of rage, I decided that instead of trying to tweak the book with improved grammar, or attempting to rephrase poor sentence structure, I would only highlight the material that stood out as spectacular.

I began actively searching for my best work.

I knew it was buried deep in the text; I just needed to find it. After I highlighted my best material, I cut the rest, removing every word that was not worthy of a green pen.

In the process, the overall book length was cut in half. A few chapters were eliminated. Other chapters went from more than twenty pages down to two paragraphs.

What remained was a small selection of high-quality text. It was not ready for publication yet, but I was significantly closer to my goal of creating a book worth reading.

You may not be working on your next best-selling novel, but I bet your life could use some fancy green pens. You and I both know where we need to improve. We hear it from our boss, our spouse, our preacher, the television, and even our best friends.

What we often miss is what makes us remarkable. Our successes are so often overshadowed by our mistakes that we use the vast majority of our brain (and spend the vast majority of our time) consumed with negativity.

Your goals will ideally represent the very best you have to offer. Your goals will challenge you to become a higher and better version of you by focusing on your strengths, natural talents, and innate passions.

If we identify what works well, and duplicate that to the extreme, we get extremely powerful results. Use your green pen as you analyze your life, work, and goals. Uncover the brilliance that is already there and bring it out to shine.

Your green pen is one secret weapon you now have to narrow your choices on what matters most in your life.

- Where are you excelling right now?
- What parts of your life are succeeding beyond your expectations?
- What are you truly grateful for, but seem to overlook in the face of so much else going on all the time?

5. ANALYZE YOUR RESULTS

It is time to take a deep dive into your responses on the Self-Evaluation, as well as the results of your Time Audit.

Self-evaluation

1. Physical Health
2. Energy
3. Relationships
4. Career and Business
5. Finances
6. Productivity
7. Grand Goals

Carefully review your responses to each question in every category.

- Where are you now?
- How do you feel about your progress in each area?
- Which areas stand out as successful and accomplished? Which areas need some serious work?

Then, consider the potential for each area, focusing on clarifying what matters most now.

- Where do you want to be in each area ten years from now?
- Which one area is the absolute most important for you to give your full attention to?
- Which one area, if dramatically improved, could have a positive impact on every other area?

Time audit

Review the data you collected during Phase I of your Time Audit.

- Where did you spend the majority of your time?
- How much time did you spend on nonessential activities?
- What is the most obvious change that can be made to free up time and allow for more productivity?

6. COMMIT TO YOUR VITAL FEW

Let's review.

You have defined your values, set your vision, reviewed your responsibilities, discovered where you are excelling using your green pen, and analyzed your Self-Evaluation and Time Audit results.

This is a large amount of data that should provide phenomenal clarity on where you are today and what you want for tomorrow.

Now is your time to commit to your vital few goals—the ambitious pursuits that will define what you focus on in the coming weeks. This is not a permanent decision, so try not to get hung up on perfectionism.

Whatever you choose now can be changed.

However, based upon the work you have already done, you likely already know exactly what matters most now. It is probably staring you right in the face.

If not, go back and review your data again. Look over your evaluation results with a close friend. Share your thoughts with someone you trust and get their opinion on your next best move.

The vital few goals you choose now will be used to build your schedule and, ultimately, will determine how your time is best utilized.

To guarantee more free time, we first need to guarantee that the bulk of your time is optimized with the fewest number of activities that bring the best results.

7. TIME AUDIT: PHASE II

Darren Hardy, the former publisher of *SUCCESS* Magazine, made a dramatic shift in his early twenties with his career in real estate. He realized he was doing everything backward.

With a stopwatch in hand, Darren timed himself to see how long he was spending each day on his most important tasks: pitching a listing, negotiating a contract, and prospecting.

On the first day, he totaled out at just nineteen minutes and fifty-four seconds.

Appalled, he decided to increase that number little by little until he was spending a significant part of each day doing his most important work, and getting the dramatic increase in results he expected.

His plan worked. His business boomed, and he went on to develop a highly profitable career in real estate—far surpassing his more experienced peers.

Using a stopwatch, Darren was able to quantify exactly how much time he was spending on his cleared-defined priority (Hardy, 2016).

Now that you have defined your vital few goals, it is time for you to do the same and double-check your progress with Phase II of the Time Audit

Phase II: subjectively, how much time is being spent on your top goals?

Just as before, choose your recording device and a day on your calendar. Get out your stopwatch and calculate the amount of time you spent on your vital few goals.

Once you know how much actual time is being spent on the vital few things that you claim matter most, you can then incrementally increase that number, and incrementally increase your results.

QUICK REVIEW: *THE VITAL FEW*

1. **There is no such thing as having multiple priorities.**
   We can truly only ever do one thing at a time, and in any given moment we only have one task that is at the top of the list. We may have many tasks we would like to accomplish over the course of the next twenty-four hours, but only one task is the supreme task right now.
2. **Clarifying what matters most is a process you can methodically complete.**
   Sometimes what matters most is obvious, but often it is quite challenging to articulate what the best use of our time should be. When you follow the steps, you can collect helpful

information that paints a clear picture of your vital few
goals in this season.

3. **The more you know about yourself and what you want, the
easier it is to pinpoint the projects that deserve your attention.**
Spending quality time reviewing your values and vision for
the future can greatly enhance your confidence in how to best
approach scheduling your day.

CHAPTER 3 ACTION PLAN

1. **Analyze the results of your Self-Evaluation and Time Audit.**
Review your responses to each question of the Evaluation,
noting areas where you feel confident, as well as notable
areas that could be significantly improved. Note in your
Time Audit where you spent the majority of your time, and
any time blocks that appear to be off track.

2. **Clarify your vital few goals to focus on in this season.**
Write down the one or two grand goals that will direct the
majority of your focus in the coming weeks. These goals will
become your filter for deciding how to best utilize your time.

3. **Complete Phase II of the Time Audit and analyze your results.**
After recording what matters most to you, find out how much
time you actually spend working on those goals. If you find
that the results are not ideal, make a plan to improve your
schedule in the following week. Focus on crafting guaranteed
blocks of time for your vital few objectives.

4

Knowing What to Do Next

Triage

Put yourself in this scenario.

It is Tuesday morning at 8:00 a.m., you just clocked in for the day and have a hot cup of coffee in hand. You sit down at your desk, and you realize a storm is brewing. There is a mountain of work to do.

Your email inbox is overflowing with messages, your phone is already blowing up with texts and calls, your calendar is overbooked, and there is a line at your door of customers, coworkers, and comanagers who need to talk to you.

What are you going to do next? How do you make that decision? You have a lot to do, and this is not a new scenario. You are a busy person and frequently find yourself flooded with more stuff than anyone could manage at one time, let alone a single day, week, or month.

The work just never ends. Your mind becomes clogged with questions that are devoid of clear answers.

- What is my next best move?
- What is my most important priority?
- What needs my attention right now?
- What can I let go of?
- What can I postpone?
- What can I eliminate forever?
- How can I not drown in this sea of pandemonium?

Fortunately, you do have many options—some are better than others, but something has to be done to address these repeated chaotic conditions.

1. **Do nothing.** Freeze. Check Facebook. Avoid the work altogether. Hope someone else solves the chaos for you.
2. **Pick something at random and go.** Get started immediately so that you feel accomplished by checking tasks off your to-do list.
3. **Let your habits kick in.** Do whatever you normally do when things get busy, despite the fact that your habits tend to lean toward quick wins and easy solutions (ignoring the elephants in the room).
4. **Answer emails.** Focus on whatever popped up since last night.
5. **Open your office door.** Talk to every person who walks in with a question.
6. **Look at your calendar.** Trust you scheduled your day appropriately.
7. **Ignore whatever is going on.** Focus on your most important big goal (despite the consequences that come with ignoring the new work).

8. **Take a walk to clear your head.** Attempt to clarify what your move should be.
9. **Implement military triage.** Sort your casualties to rationally allocate your limited resources.
10. **Put out the biggest fires first.** Hope you do not start any new ones in the process.

This list is not comprehensive. There are other options, but ultimately you will have to decide how to filter what gets done, and in what order.

Not everything will be addressed. Many things will never be accomplished—ever. You will have to choose for yourself. Every scenario is different, and there is no one best answer for all situations, or especially for your situation right now.

Ultimately, the best answer lies in developing the skill of being able to quickly prioritize the vital few tasks while postponing absolutely everything else. As time progresses, you will develop a highly useful toolbox of prioritization strategies.

In this chapter, we will discuss five stages of prioritization for your ongoing projects, as well as a variety of strategies to filter your ideas and requests for your time, so you know how to handle the true urgency and importance of the work landing on your desk.

THE FIVE STAGES OF PROJECT PRIORITIZATION

I tend to get overly ambitious.

I take on projects when any new idea pops into my head, or I read about a fun strategy that appears vitally important for my business, or I attend a conference and take pages and pages of notes with more stuff to do than I will ever have time for.

For years, I would not write down the new ideas in any organized system. I would just begin tackling the new projects immediately, simply adding them to my ever-expanding workload.

At some point, I would realize the number of projects I committed to was growing too fast. I would pause and write all of them down to craft a comprehensive list of everything I was committed to accomplishing.

These lists became my go-to for project management.

Initially, they were incredibly helpful because I had visual clarity over the various promises I had made to myself and others.

However, it became apparent over time that simply acknowledging I was too busy to ever get everything done was not enough.

You cannot simply say, "Here are the 124 goals I have for the next ninety days."

That is not progress—it is insanity—and it is undeniably overwhelming and counterproductive.

The breakthrough came when I began to distinctly classify my projects. I created clear categories for them and found systematic approaches to ignore everything that was not vitally important in my current season.

These classifications have proven their worth time and time again, especially during the busiest of seasons. When you have committed to too much, your next action is clear and written down right in front of you.

When you have cleared enough free space that you feel confident you can take on more work, your next action is clear and written down right in front of you.

Clarity to this degree is beautiful and rare.

Knowing what matters most, seeing those items written down in a clear and compelling manner, and then making significant and tangible progress on those priorities is the epitome of being a productivity rock star.

If you truly want more freedom, more free time, or more margin in your life to pursue what matters most, organizing your life and business with well-designed systems is not just imperative—it is as close to a mandate as you will ever hear from me.

Here is a description of the Five Stages of Project Prioritization.

1. Stage zero: no priority

Stage Zero provides no priority at all. These are your future projects that will get none of your attention in this season.

Zero.

These are your future ideas, bucket list fantasies, anything you cannot or should not do now. Ninety-five percent of your ideas and projects will be in this category.

In fact, you may have to eventually create subcategories for these ideas if you find yourself with dozens or hundreds of potential pursuits.

Projects in this stage will only progress to future stages when they have proven themselves to be significant and truly worthy of your time. The bar is high and very few projects will ever make it out of Stage Zero.

2. Stage one: low priority

Stage One consists of your lowest priority projects, those that are important but not urgent.

Projects in this stage will likely consist of goals that you can or have to do very slowly over time. Think of these as requiring minimum payments, like a long-term loan that you will eventually pay off—but not anytime soon.

This stage could include goals that require small, recurring investments over time, but likely nothing significant all at once. This could include long-term goals around your health, financial investments, networking, or anything that you know needs to be addressed in bite-sized pieces.

3. Stage two: medium priority

Stage Two consists of your middle-of-the-road projects, those you need to monitor closely but which may not require you to devote any significant time in the next couple of weeks.

Medium priority projects consist of ones that have looming deadlines and could surprise you if you find yourself procrastinating on them.

These are the most dangerous because we often find ourselves shocked that we forget to do anything about these projects until the very last minute.

It is wise to schedule recurring reminders to work on these projects every one to two weeks to avoid any stressful moments leading up to the cut-off time.

4. Stage three: high priority

Stage Three projects are your vital few, the same few (or just one) that you identified in the last chapter.

These projects will consist of your current most important work. This is the number one focus in your life at this moment, your one singular objective.

I highly encourage you to leave only enough space for a single project in this category at any one time. The more you attempt to prioritize as urgent and important, the less likely either of those qualifiers is true.

5. Stage four: Armageddon

The final stage, Stage Four, is your last resort.

If any project lands in this category, you will know it because it will consume 100 percent of your attention. These are emergencies: world-ending, heart-stopping, Armageddon-esque problems.

Projects that qualify as worthy of Stage Four could include heart attacks, bankruptcies, house fires, your website crashing in the middle of a product launch, or any other situation that stops everything else in its tracks.

These could also include wonderful opportunities, like the birth of a child, your wedding day, or skydiving for the first time (believe me, nothing else matters when you are free-falling at 140 miles per hour straight toward the earth).

ORGANIZING AND UPDATING THE STATUS OF YOUR PROJECTS

On a practical level, I use Evernote (a digital notebook) to organize, monitor, and update my projects. Feel free to use any note-taking system that you are already comfortable with and are actively using.

The only requirement is that you use the system you claim to use. That may sound obvious, but I know way too many people who "use" Evernote, but have not updated it for years.

Schedule time on your calendar at least once a week to thoroughly review the status of your projects. It will not take long after your system has been set up.

If you are keeping a short leash on the number of projects you pursue at any one time, this process will be quick, simple, and quite helpful.

Too many great ideas

Sometimes your greatest enemy to productivity is the onslaught of too many great ideas to consider and opportunities to pursue.

Many people that I meet think about productivity in one specific manner. They envision using strategies to accomplish more tasks on a to-do list, which equates to just being busier with more work they do not want to do (think: *my boss just assigned me more tasks to complete, and now I have to figure out how to get it all done*).

However, when I think about productivity, I picture something completely different, accomplishing amazing projects—*many* amazing projects of my choosing in both my work and personal life.

In my work as a speaker, author, and podcaster, generating new ideas to share is part of my job description. However, due to my passion for personal development, I love getting new ideas that will enhance my work and life in any way.

I am sure you can relate.

Think back to the last passion project you took on (e.g., running a marathon, designing your new home, learning a new language, building a new business).

When the project began, and you started to see the potential for it to go well, you likely went through a period where your excitement took over.

You started to picture all of the many ways you could tackle the goal: the supplies you would need, the people you would meet, the other opportunities you would generate because of this new project.

Excitement at that level is often what I love most about my life. Getting a new idea is as great a high as anything I have experienced because it puts me in a euphoric state of positive hope, potential, and possibility.

When you stay in that state long enough, you begin to get many new ideas—so many in fact, that you end up with too many.

Filtering your many ideas down to the vital few you will have time to pursue is challenging. We addressed this issue in part in the last chapter, as well as with the Five Stages of Project Prioritization, but take a few minutes to consider how else you could narrow your choices.

How else could you create your short list of high-priority projects that would change your life forever?

Thirteen strategies to filter your ideas and decide what to do next

1. Big Picture Planning.

Using the results from your Self-Evaluation in chapter 2, consider the big picture of your life. How do you want to live on a daily basis, and what goals would enable that vision? What does your lifestyle look like in an ideal sense, and what would it take to bring that to reality?

2. Game-Changing Qualifiers.

Is your new project idea a game-changing goal that must be pursued to the exclusion of everything else? How many of your ideas fall into this bucket? How many of your goals, if accomplished successfully, would change your entire life forever?

3. Must-Dos.

Is your new idea necessary or required to move another goal forward? What consequences, if any, would you experience if this goal was never accomplished?

4. Remarkable Results.

Will your new idea directly or indirectly generate significant results? Sometimes an idea is worth pursuing simply because it will improve your life so much that you cannot imagine backing down now. Does your new idea rise to the occasion?

5. Too Easy to Pass Up.

Could your new idea be completed so quickly, easily, or with such minimal effort that you may as well just do it? There are many small goals that are worthy of your time if they can be wrapped up swiftly. Are you better off just getting it done so you can move on?

6. Do What Is Obvious. Do What Is Right.

For years I used the phase, "do what is obvious, do what is right," when I found myself stuck at a fork in the road. Is your new goal obviously the right decision? Is your new idea so clear that you would regret not doing it?

7. Ask Around.

Other people often know us better than we know ourselves. Have you asked anyone else about your new idea? Who could you speak with that would provide wisdom and clarity to your situation?

8. Raise the Bar.

On the vision board in my office I have a large piece of paper with this phrase in bold marker, "Is it a 9 or 10? No? Walk away." We often consider ideas that are good, but not great. If your new goal would not qualify as a nine or ten, is it worth your time? Would it be considered high-end, professional, or superior in quality?

9. **Apply the WOW Factor.**

Is your new idea a BIG project and would it WOW someone? When I first fell in love with distance running, I fell in love with the idea of impressing myself, which I used to challenge my limiting beliefs about how far and fast I could run. Does your new idea impress you? Is it a WOW project? Does it exceed your bar of excellence?

10. **Get Out Your T-Chart.**

Listing pros and cons of a complex project may sound simple, but clarity does not lie. Knowing and writing down exactly why a new idea is great, and why it is not, will make the decision infinitely easier.

11. **Consider the Web of Impact.**

Will your goal eliminate the need to pursue other goals in the future? Sometimes a goal can have a tremendous impact across many areas, making other goals nearly unnecessary. Will your goal pack a punch?

12. **Pause.**

Meditation, prayer, or contemplation are all useful strategies for letting an idea sit for a minute so you can make an educated decision. Rushing a new idea into existence may be the wrong strategy. Could your goal be implemented more intelligently if you gave it time to mature?

13. **Go Now.**

The best solution to decide whether or not to pursue a new idea is not to wait at all. Try it and see what happens. Clarity is often best achieved in hindsight, and many ideas only make sense after implementation. Could the best strategy be to just jump in feet first?

QUICK REVIEW: *KNOWING WHAT TO DO NEXT*

1. Prioritization is a skill you can master.

Knowing what matters most at any point in time is subjective, but the power is in your hands. When you develop a large toolbox of productivity strategies, you provide yourself the means to tackle anything that comes your way.

2. Classifying the priority of your current and future projects provides unrivaled clarity.

By using the Five Stages of Project Prioritization, you can determine the importance of each of your current and future goals with amazing precision. Ninety-five percent of your goals will be in Stage Zero, meaning they will be classified as completely deprioritized future goals.

3. You have more than a dozen strategies at your disposal to filter your opportunities, ideas, and projects.

Some projects are clearly important whereas others may not be as obvious. When you ask the right questions, you can quickly determine which goals are worth your time, and which can wait for later.

CHAPTER 4 ACTION PLAN

1. Prioritize your projects.

Using the Five Stages of Project Prioritization, determine the importance of each of your major projects and goals. Most goals can wait until later, and they will have to, in order to make room for what matters most.

2. Post a list of strategies to filter your ideas.

On the vision board in my office, I have a list of filters to help clarify what to do next. Create your short list of the best filters that work for you and post them in a visible location where you work.

3. **Use pressure when it suits you.**

   Some tasks are best tackled at the last minute, and you may be the kind of person who thrives under pressure. If so, let the act of procrastinating work in your favor to ensure you get the work done that truly is urgent and important.

STEP

III

Flex Your Muscles

5

Fitness for Busy People

Adopt a Health-First Approach

Your health is more important than your résumé, checklist, bucket list, or achievement ranking system.

Adopting a health-first approach is a sure-fire strategy to guarantee you can achieve your most ambitious goals far into the future.

I am as guilty of neglecting this as anyone.

Over the last few years, I have noticed a trend in my habits and calendaring methods: I am good at prioritizing work or working out, but never both at the same time.

During one season, I can exercise like a champ six to seven days a week, lose weight, build muscle, and feel better than ever.

In another season, I can wake up early and dominate my task list, getting more work accomplished in a few hours than most do all day.

However, it appears that these two seasons have always remained independent. There is little or no overlap, and I wind up either being in the best shape of my life or making tremendous growth in my work, but not both.

This is silly.

It is not only possible to remain healthy while pursuing your goals, but it is also the only way you will be able to pursue them long term.

Think of it this way, if you do not adopt a health-first approach, where does health fall on your list of priorities? When will you take care of yourself? When will you eat better, get off the couch and go the gym, or stop smoking?

If health is not number one, where is it?

When anything supersedes your physical and mental health, you take a hit. You withdraw from your health savings account, so to speak.

Additionally, to ensure you have free time on your calendar, a few things must be true:

1. You must accomplish a smaller number of important goals faster.
2. You must have the physical capacity to do the work in the first place.

Without your health, you have nothing. Without taking care of yourself, your free time will not be free—it will cost a tremendous amount in lost hours spent playing catch up.

You can accomplish your ambitious goals AND be incredibly healthy. Both are possible with a simple plan and a burning desire to live like you never have before.

STEP III: FLEX YOUR MUSCLES

The third step of *The Free-Time Formula* is to flex your muscles, and it is divided into two parts: fitness for busy people and mental bicep curls.

This is where you begin to truly enjoy the fruits of your labor because you will have the energy, enthusiasm, and mental clarity to pursue not only your current goals but even bigger dreams yet to come.

Small Changes, Big Results

1. Taking Care of Number One
2. Fitness for Busy People
3. Intensity versus Mediocrity
4. Top Daily Healthy Habits
5. One Year No Beer

Clarity of Thought

1. Pausing Is Productive
2. Pausing on Purpose
3. Mental Bicep Curls
4. Finding a Moment to Pause

I am not a doctor, personal trainer, or medical professional. Consider the health recommendations in this book as ideas or possibilities to pursue—not direct medical advice. Please consult with your physician for customized diet and fitness plans.

Taking care of number one

There are few things, if any, that I value more than my health.

More than my work, more than my goals, more than my relationship with my wife, I value taking care of myself to the best of my ability.

Why?

Because without my health I will not have the capacity to work, accomplish goals, or give myself fully to my closest relationships.

Your health is your ticket to *everything*.

In a very literal sense, without your health you are dead. How much work do you plan to accomplish at the cemetery?

This is not a trite question—I mean it. How do you plan to stay happy, focused, and productive when your mind and body are failing you?

Fatigue, stress, and burnout are only a few examples of physical reactions you may experience when pushing too hard or simply avoiding the replenishing work that brings you back to life.

Eating healthy foods, working out, and sleeping soundly are widely known but extraordinarily undervalued life-producing strategies.

There was a season of my life in my mid-twenties that I frequently think about because it stands out as the healthiest season of my life. I made radical changes to my diet, lost weight, began running marathons at a vigorous pace, and had more energy than at any point I can remember.

I had a trim waistline, a passion for hitting the trails whenever I could, and enthusiasm for just about everything because I just felt so good, so often.

The changes I made were simple. The "work" I put in was not unmanageable, and it rarely felt like work at all.

I was exploring parks, signing up for races, trying new foods, and experimenting with a health-first approach that proved again and again to be the best choice for my life, goals, and morale that I had ever made.

Prioritizing *me* was no longer an afterthought, but instead was becoming my go-to strategy for living my best life.

In the Introduction of this book, I told a rough story of my trip to the emergency room. This event not only served as a staunch wake-up call to me that I had let my priorities slip, but that there are serious consequences for doing so.

My goal is to help you free up time for what matters most, and I firmly believe that one of the best ways to carve out more time on your calendar—and optimize the time you already have—is to be in the best shape of your life.

Repeatedly engaging in life-enhancing activities, those that bring about more energy, passion, and enthusiasm, is the secret to living a more full and productive life.

When your time is filled with projects that boost your spirit, you may also find that you are less inclined to waste the free time you already have. In other words, couch-potato time is less sexy when you could be climbing mountains, surfing ocean waves, or kayaking through the Grand Canyon.

- When in your life were you in peak condition?
- When do you frequently feel at your best, and what causes that to happen?
- What physical activities light you up and boost your energy?
- What bad habits have you acquired recently that are blocking your road to greater health, energy, and vitality?
- What have you been ignoring for years that you know would bring you back to your best self?
- What's the first thing you do when you wake up in the morning?
- What activities tend to crowd out what you want to spend your time on?

As a busy person, I can imagine that you may be inclined to think that I am recommending you spend hours a day in the gym or preparing complex healthy meals, when in fact this process can (and should) be so much easier.

Instead of thinking about all of the many ways you could get healthy, or what professional athletes do to reach their optimal state, think about how to pack the biggest punch in the smallest time frame.

Freeing up time means allowing every precious moment to reach its highest potential. You can exercise for ten minutes and make real progress. You can eat healthier foods instead of diving into your normal meal. You can eliminate one small task a day and replace it with a healthier alternative.

You can get incredible value in small doses if you play your cards right.

Focus on doing the fewest number of healthy activities that you can to improve your current situation. Make it your goal to get as much value from every minute as you can.

I see too many people engaging in pointless exercises at the gym, or simply socializing, instead of maximizing the precious time they have to get the results they came there to acquire.

As you free up more time on your calendar and improve your energy, you can "up your game" and increase the intensity. Starting slow and small is best to build the habit of movement as you embrace a health-first approach.

Small habits can become large, powerful, and enormously effective with time.

Today, start small but make it count. Little victories can produce tremendous outcomes.

Fitness for busy people

If you are too busy to work out, you are too busy. This is my mantra and one you can feel free to adopt.

Ideally, you should have time on most days for three essential activities:

1. Physical fitness

Daily movement is one thing, intelligently accelerating your heart rate, flexing your muscles, and actively managing your physical well-being is something else. It does not take multiple hours of your time each day to be fit. You can make a big difference with a small, but well-chosen, set of movements.

2. Working on your craft

Being busy is never the goal—making direct progress on your vital few goals is a much better approach that leads to tremendous results down the road. With a short but well-chosen task list, you can consistently advance your position in whatever you choose to pursue.

3. Enjoying the fruits of your labor

Free time can be stress-free time. When you have taken care of your work, and yourself, you will have the capacity, energy, and time on your calendar to be fully present and alert for whatever activities you choose to pursue.

If you do not have time for all three of these on a recurring basis, you are too busy, or your priorities are out of order.

The goal is not necessarily to guarantee time for all three of these activities seven days a week, but aiming for five to six would create a solid rhythm.

The fabricated trade-off: exercise time versus productivity time

Exercise time does not replace productivity time; it enhances it.

If you operate with the false belief that time spent working out is time spent NOT checking items off your to-do list, your to-do list or your workout routine is too long, or both.

There is an ideal and flexible weekly routine we are aiming for if our goal is to ensure time for our vital few goals AND exercise.

There is a rhythm that can be achieved on your calendar that allows you the opportunity to take care of yourself and your most important work each day.

The key is a health-first approach. I cannot see your calendar at the moment, so I cannot coach you through how your exact circumstances will ebb and flow around your workout goals.

However, I can tell you that if you booked work on your calendar first, and tried to squeeze in exercise in the margins, you are doing it backward. A health-first approach means scheduling your "me time" first, and everything else outside that time.

Taking into account that you likely have prescheduled on-the-clock hours with your employer, and other essentials in your life, the approach still holds true.

As soon as something replaces health on your calendar as the most important objective, your health slips.

This is a hard pill to swallow; I get it. Your mind is likely racing with arguments why this approach cannot work for you, or anyone with a job, kids, or other highly important obligations.

So, think of this way, if you continue to do what you have been doing, will you get the results you want?

No? Then it is time for a new approach.

A health-first approach is a mindset strategy first and a scheduling strategy second. Let that idea sink in, and when you are on board, take another look at your calendar.

What can move? What can be postponed? What are you doing now that you do not absolutely have to do?

If exercise was nonnegotiable (e.g., my doctor told me I had to exercise for thirty minutes every day), what would have to change to make that possible?

The answers may not appear right away, so hold this thought until we tackle cutting the nonsense in Step IV. Scheduling is an ongoing challenge, but there is always something that can be done—*always*.

Your new fitness plan: quick, but powerful

Guaranteeing fitness time for busy people means making the very most of the few precious minutes you have available.

If you have ten minutes, you have enough to begin. Consider these two approaches with your next workout session.

1. Strength Training

If you are going to lift weights, lift hard and then stop.

Michael Matthews, author of the popular fitness books *Bigger, Leaner, Stronger: The Simple Science of Building the Ultimate Male Body* and *Thinner, Leaner, Stronger: The Simple Science of Building the Ultimate Female Body*, advocates many effective strategies, four of which are notable with our focus on minimizing time and maximizing results (Matthews, 2015).

1. **Use impeccable form** to ensure you do not injure yourself. I am speaking from years of personal experience here and dozens of injuries to back it up. Form matters more than anything, and nothing wastes more time than sitting on the bench with a doctor's note.
2. **When possible, use free weights,** or you own bodyweight, instead of using machines. Free weights provide a more powerful and effective lift as you activate many more muscles per movement.
3. **Focus on compound movements** instead of isolation exercises. Compound exercises, like the squat, deadlift, and bench press, activate multiple muscle groups and build your

whole body faster than attempting to lift each muscle group one at a time.

4. **Use the principle of progressive tension overload,** which means *"progressively increasing tension levels in the muscle fibers over time. That is, lifting progressively heavier and heavier weights"* (Matthews 2015, 28). Growth over time is the goal, and slowly increasing the challenge is what causes your muscles to continue to develop.

If you want to build strength and save time, these simple strategies will point you in the right direction. For more information and clarity on these principles, I highly recommend reading Matthews' books.

2. Interval Training

Intensity beats mediocrity, especially when it comes to cardiovascular fitness.

I spent years running marathons, and my own experience proved that the days I pushed hard were the days I grew. The days I ran at a moderate pace without challenging myself were the days I stayed busy but went nowhere.

The goal here is not to train for an endurance race—those take significant time per week, and per workout. The goal is to boost our level of fitness quickly, and then hit the showers and move on with our work for the day.

Interval training is a highly effective cardiovascular workout that requires a tiny fraction of the time you may be envisioning.

The key is to focus on a quick rhythm, pushing hard for a short period and then backing off significantly. For example, you could sprint for thirty seconds, and then slow jog for sixty seconds, repeating that set a few times.

The total workout could be no more than fifteen minutes, and yet you have the potential to make tremendous progress.

Sprinting is intense, and requires a strong base of athletic fitness. If you are currently not in great shape, build up your foundation slowly over time before pushing too hard, too fast.

High-Intensity Interval Training (HIIT), trail running, and other forms of exercise that focus on the rhythm of pushing hard and then pausing . . . pushing hard and then pausing, return phenomenal results in significantly less time than what many of us do when we work out.

The Free-Time Formula mantra for fitness is clear: minimize time and maximize results by pushing yourself and then resting. Work hard and then play hard—you have earned it.

MOST PRODUCTIVE DAILY HEALTHY HABITS

As a busy high achiever, adopting a few key habits (while simultaneously limiting your most destructive ones) is a powerful strategy to squeeze more time out of your day without radically changing your entire life.

To supplement your daily workout, adding or removing the right habits will help boost your productivity and health in a big way.

1. Take in just enough caffeine.

I have a love-hate relationship with caffeine. I love it as much as it helps me, which lasts until the tables turn and I find myself stuck in a jittery chaotic loop or a useless afternoon slump. If you choose to consume caffeine, carefully study its true effect on your whole life and its impact on your focus, sleep, energy levels, stress levels, mood, dietary choices, and actual productivity output.

2. **Eat plenty of nutrient-dense foods and hydrate.**
You are going to eat, so you may as well eat healthy food to boost your energy and feel your best all day long. When planning your day, plan to only allow yourself access to nutrient-dense foods and plenty of clean water to boost your energy. I often pack a bag full of fresh produce when I travel or leave the house to work so that I am not limited to vending machines or fast-food restaurants. I am choosing the green pepper or the banana, the blueberries or the peaches, the purified water or the orange juice.

3. **Draw clear boundaries around sleep.**
Setting strict limitations on the hours you allow yourself to work will directly affect the hours you allow yourself to get high-quality rest each night. Your overall health is affected tremendously by how well you sleep, which makes it imperative to prioritize getting to sleep on time or early every night.

4. **Cut out your vices.**
I frequently challenge myself to let go of my addictions on a regular basis to see the true impact of my choices on my daily health and productivity. If you need a break from alcohol, junk food, or surfing the Internet, try a detox day. The quick results of giving up a single vice for just twenty-four hours can spark new momentum and have a profound effect on your daily habits moving forward.

5. Review your habits.

One of the best ways to ensure you stick to the key habits you have chosen is to adopt the habit of reviewing your habits. Begin by analyzing the results of your habits on a daily basis, determining which habits were effective and which were not, which habits you stuck to and which you found an excuse for, which habits were easy to maintain and which were challenging to accomplish.

QUICK REVIEW: *FITNESS FOR BUSY PEOPLE*

1. Your health is your ticket to everything.

Repeatedly engaging in life-enhancing activities, those that bring about more energy, passion, and enthusiasm, is the secret to living a more full and productive life. When your time is filled with projects that boost your spirit, energy, and overall health, you may also find that you are less inclined to waste the free time you already have.

2. If you are too busy to work out, you are too busy.

Ideally, you should have time on most days for three essential activities: physical fitness, working on your craft, and enjoying the fruits of your labor. If you do not have time for all three of these on a recurring basis, you are too busy, or your priorities are out of order.

3. Adopt the most effective habits.

As a busy high achiever, adopting a few key habits (while simultaneously limiting your most destructive ones), is a powerful strategy to squeeze more time out of your day without radically changing your entire life. To supplement your daily workout, adding or removing the right habits will help boost your productivity and health in a big way.

CHAPTER 5 ACTION PLAN

1. Adopt a health-first approach.

If you are going to continue your high-achievement lifestyle for the foreseeable future, you will not get far without your health. Taking care of yourself is not only a priority, but it is also an absolute necessity, or your goals will never get done. Defeating recurring stress, overwhelm, and anxiety are dependent upon you managing your health alongside your responsibilities.

2. Guarantee a little time for fitness every single day.

If you are too busy to work out, you are too busy. It does not take much—even as little as ten (intense) minutes a day can make a dramatic difference in your energy and level of fitness. Of course, you can feel free to do more than ten minutes, but start there and see where it gets you.

3. Let go of one vice.

We all have them, and they hold us back more than we realize. It could be alcohol, junk food, TV, or some other bad habit that is creeping into your life and preventing you from having the abundance of energy, vitality, and enthusiasm you know you could have. Try letting one thing go for a week and track your results. Significant transformation begins with tiny changes.

6

Mental Bicep Curls

Pausing Is Productive

If there is any physical activity I enjoy more than running, it is backpacking.

A few years ago, I took a trip with my father and brother to Yellowstone National Park with the intention of doing a few touristy activities, and then spending the bulk of our time hiking, camping, and climbing mountains.

This trip came at an ideal time for me. I had been incredibly busy at work and had given myself very little time for decompressing.

A big part of me was thrilled to be detaching from the hustle and bustle of daily life to find a new rhythm, if only for a few days. A smaller part of me was concerned this excursion would serve as nothing more than a delay in productivity, a ten-day obstacle between me and my goals.

What I missed then, and what is utterly apparent today, was that *this trip was the goal.*

This adventure into the wilderness was life at its best—not a distraction from checking more boxes on yet another list.

As the backpacking began, what surprised me most was my initial inability to soak up the beauty all around me. Sure, I was taking lots of pictures, but I was in no way present.

I was still mentally and digitally connected to my life back at home, checking email, social media, and website stats (*which I still check way too often today*).

As the trip continued to unfold, I slowly began to find myself thinking more about blisters and potential bear attacks than missed email or opportunities to do more work at the office.

I was unwinding, bit by bit.

On the fourth day, we scaled to the top of a mountain and took some of the most beautiful pictures I can imagine. Though I was experiencing mild altitude sickness and fighting to stay hydrated, I was finally there.

I was truly in Yellowstone for the first time.

I was living out each moment, eating each powdered food packet with enthusiasm, and dreaming about how I could live in the mountains for weeks or months, instead of days.

It took a solid ninety-six hours of hauling around sixty pounds of gear on my back, but I got there.

I was alert, present, and content with each moment, despite the obvious challenges of not showering, sleeping on the ground, and gripping my bear mace canister like my life depended on it (*you know, because it did*).

At the best moments of the trip, I was doing very little. I would sit and watch. I would listen. I would breathe. I would just let life happen to me, instead of the other way around.

These moments were life changing. They were revealing my weaknesses, tendencies, bad habits, and deep mental ruts.

I was opening up part of me that I normally keep hidden beneath piles of paperwork and ever-evolving ambitious pursuits. I was, for the first time in years, experiencing the immense beauty of life without having to force it into being.

It finally dawned on me that pausing is healthy and productive.

Breaks between activities are activities themselves, and they may be more valuable than any goal I could ever pursue.

PAUSING ON PURPOSE

We need a break.

We need time to slow down and build ourselves back up, time to breathe life back into us, time to refill and rebuild.

I am highly skilled at staying busy. I can find something to do anywhere I go, and I can normally find something productive to accomplish in any situation.

As someone who values productivity, high achievement, and staying active as often as possible, I have found that pausing in the heart of a busy season, or a busy day, is one of the most difficult challenges I face.

However, there is immense value in the pause, in intentionally slowing the pace of the day, or in simply stopping to consciously take a breath after an intense and productive session.

If you are striving to add more free time to your calendar or to simply enjoy more of the free time you already have, learning to pause effectively can help in dramatic ways.

Benefits of an intentional pause

1. You remember to breathe deeply.

We are shallow when it comes to breathing, which is why you will hear a yoga or meditation teacher begin a class by directly asking you to take a few deep breaths. We generally do not breathe deeply from our diaphragm unless we are told to do so. Intentionally pausing when you are busy gives you the opportunity to breathe deeply, relax, and de-stress.

2. You connect the dots.

Good ideas float to the surface when you stop trying so hard. If achieving pristine mental clarity is important to you, then giving your brain the chance to relax and connect ideas will help a great deal. Going for a walk in the middle of the day, pausing to regroup after pushing hard, or taking a few minutes to meditate and stretch can have profound effects on your ability to experience more epiphanies and aha moments.

3. You loosen your grip.

Do you ever catch yourself clenching your fist, and then have to consciously tell yourself to relax your muscles? This happens to me when I am pushing too hard and have not given myself the chance to calm down. Pausing can not only heal these tense moments, but it can also prevent them from happening altogether.

MENTAL BICEP CURLS

One of the greatest methods I have found to effectively pause, clarify my thoughts, and deeply relax is through meditation.

During a busy winter season, I took a six-week meditation class that had a profound effect on me right when I needed it the most. Each class lasted forty-five minutes and focused on listening to the slow humming sound of Tibetan singing bowls.

No matter how I entered each class (happy or angry, content or stressed out) I always left feeling a deep sense of calm and fulfillment. Each session could have lasted twice as long, and I would likely have loved each one even more.

For most of my life, I convinced myself that I could not meditate, that it was impossible to stop all of my thoughts, and that because I was so hyped up all the time, I would likely be a terrible monk.

As it turns out, I was wrong on all counts. Thanks to a little research I discovered I was approaching meditation completely backward: we can all meditate, stopping your thoughts is not possible or the goal of meditation, and (let's get real) I was never trying to become a monk in the first place.

Dan Harris, a news anchor and author of the book *10% Happier*, experienced a panic attack while live on national television (Harris 2014, 1). Due to a highly demanding job, significant time spent reporting in war zones, and a persistent cocaine addiction, a scary situation like this one was only a matter of time.

The panic attack served as an enormous wake-up call and one that led Harris to a healing meditation practice.

The key to his practice and the epiphany that forever changed my approach to meditation is repeatedly flexing your brain's "muscles," or performing mental bicep curls.

When most people think about meditating, they tend to envision clearing their mind of everything or thinking about nothing. Then, when they inevitably think about a million random things they assume they have failed and, therefore, cannot meditate.

The reality is that turning your brain off is not the point. Each time you veer off track, the goal is to acknowledge your stray thought and then return to your focal point (your breath, the sound of singing bowls, positive affirmations, and so on).

Like flexing and releasing the tension when you do a bicep curl, when meditating you get distracted and then you refocus, get distracted and then refocus, distracted, refocus, distracted, refocus, distracted, refocus, over and over again.

Over time, your distractions will likely occur less often, your ability to concentrate can improve dramatically, and your meditation sessions can continue without the frustration of "failing."

This is a game-changing strategy if you have concluded that meditating is not for you. I will be the first to admit that I wrote off meditation as a useful tool for "someone else, but never me."

Even five minutes a day of mental bicep curls can have a profound effect on your stress levels, concentration, and ability to find a little peace in a hectic season.

Active meditation for busy bodies

If the idea of traditional meditation is not appealing, or you want a more active form of concentration that will shake up your normal routine, there is one specific practice that may work wonders for you.

Wim Hof, known as "The Iceman," has become well known for his radical approach to health through extreme cold exposure and intense breathing techniques (Hof, 2017). He has personally accomplished incredible feats, set dozens of world records, and challenged conventional thinking through his unorthodox techniques.

I went through his ten-week course to learn the method behind the madness, so to speak, and can personally attest that his approach is nothing short of extraordinary. In just a few minutes, Wim walks you through a rapid fire series of deep breathing exercises, often followed up with cold showers or physical exercise to put your training into practice.

Wim's approach to meditation is vigorous, and his recommendations can border on extreme, but that is exactly why I find him and his methods so appealing.

Traditional approaches do not always work. Conventional methods are not for everyone.

If you want to uproot your life in ways you never expected, spend some time with Wim.

FINDING A MOMENT TO PAUSE

Consider a few strategies when attempting to find time to let go during your busiest days.

1. Just after the alarm goes off
I have interviewed hundreds of high achievers on my podcast, and one of the most common daily habits is meditation. Surprisingly, many of those same high achievers meditate while still lying in bed before they begin their day. Life gets busy as soon as your feet hit the floor. Assuming you can stay alert (without falling back asleep), consider finding your quiet time just as the sun rises.

2. Between meetings or appointments
I frequently book meetings back-to-back to save time. However, it is quite common to end up with an awkward amount of time to fill if a meeting ends a few minutes early. In the downtime, I find it incredibly beneficial to sneak in a quick session of meditation. It only takes a few minutes and can clear your head before you dive into the next work session.

3. Just after a workout
I noticed a trend with my workout routines a few years ago and then made a dramatic shift to get more value out of my

workout time. What I noticed was that I was unintentionally batching a variety of exercises together when I worked out. The opposite was also true; I would not do any of the exercises if I chose to skip a workout. For example, if I went for a run I was more likely to practice yoga right afterward. If I did not run it was highly likely that I would not practice yoga that day either. If you consistently do an activity every day (like exercise), you could tack on a quick session of quiet time to wrap up that activity. Anchoring a new habit, such as meditation, to a more consistent one you already practice is a sure-fire way to guarantee you get your new habit to stick.

4. **On vacation**

This may seem obvious, but my vacations tend to be anything but relaxing. It is common to plan a vacation where you intend to slow the pace of life, only to wind up booking so many activities that the vacation is more exhausting than anything you do all year! If your vacation is supposed to be relaxing, then relax. Schedule a few hours a day to do absolutely nothing. The odds are that you will fill that time anyway, so be firm in setting your boundaries to ensure you get the time off you need.

5. **When sitting in traffic**

This may surprise you, but I miss my daily commute. I used to drive twenty-five miles to work in the morning and twenty-five miles back home each night. That time was phenomenal for decompression, time that I do not get today as a work-from-home entrepreneur, unless I intentionally leave for an errand or meeting. Though it is obviously not advised to drive with your eyes closed, you can play calming music, listen to a meditative audio recording, or practice positive affirmations in the car.

6. **Just before you fall asleep**

In addition to meditating, nearly every one of the achievers I have interviewed read consistently. Often, the best chance to read a great book, pause for a few minutes of yoga, or say a quick prayer is just before you close your eyes at night. If the rest of your household is calming down too, this may be a great opportunity to de-stress, collect your thoughts, and fall asleep fast.

7. **In a meditation class**

Sometimes the best way to address a problem is to smack it in the face. If all else fails, sign up for a class and go. My meditation class was so effective that I proved to myself I could meditate and that meditation is one of the best strategies for stress reduction I have ever tried. Find a class near you and attend. Your calm mind will thank me later.

QUICK REVIEW: *MENTAL BICEP CURLS*

1. **Pausing is healthy and productive.**

You can experience the immense beauty of life without having to force it into being. Breaks between activities are activities themselves, and they may be more valuable than any goal you could ever pursue.

2. **We need to breathe deeply on purpose.**

We generally do not breathe deeply from our diaphragm unless we are told to do so. Intentionally pausing when you are busy gives you the opportunity to breathe deeply, relax, and de-stress.

3. **Mental bicep curls can radically alter the traditional approach to meditation.**

This is a game-changing strategy if you have concluded that meditating is not for you. Even five minutes a day of mental bicep curls can have a profound effect on your stress levels, concentration, and ability to find a little peace in a hectic season.

CHAPTER 6 ACTION PLAN

1. **Flex your mental muscles for a few minutes each day.**
   Prioritize time for mindful rejuvenation, whether that be through meditation, prayer, yoga, or another form of quiet time. Pausing amid the hustle will give you a perspective you cannot get through any other means. Practice your mental bicep curls and remember that distraction is part of the game. Acknowledge the misdirection and refocus, acknowledge and refocus... over and over again.

2. **Find your form of meditation.**
   Traditional approaches do not always work, and conventional methods are not for everyone. If you are in a rut and need a radical approach to spark new momentum and begin again, try an alternative technique. There are many effective strategies that can reduce stress and provide clarity where you need it most. Be willing to try something new when old methods no longer do the trick.

3. **Find your moment to pause.**
   There is no right or wrong moment to slow down. Schedules change, people change, and needs change. Carving out a few minutes between meetings, or just before you crawl out of bed, or just before you turn the lights off at night are all possibilities.

STEP

IV

Cut the Nonsense

7

You Have Permission to Let Go

Let It Go

Trying to do it all?

Let it go.

Maintaining a perfectly clean house?

Let it go.

Catching up on every episode of *The Bachelor*?

Cue the *Frozen* soundtrack.

If I could give you only one piece of advice to free up more time on your calendar every week, it would be to stop doing dumb, useless nonsense.

Harsh? Yes, but I would guess that you and I both engage in activities all the time that never have to happen at all.

Typically, when we think about free time, we are thinking about spending less time on the things we dislike (responsibilities, obligations, and so on), to spend more time on the things we love.

In reality, we *are* routinely spending time on things we enjoy, but those activities have a very low return on investment.

The ROI of our normal weekly habits is weak at best.

Does watching every episode of your latest TV show bring you happiness, or do you watch every episode out of some vague sense of loyalty?

Are you surfing the Internet for life-altering information that could springboard you to success, or do you scan social media sites again and again because it is more entertaining than getting back to work?

We do things all the time out of habit.

We engage in activities that are mediocre or good, but far from great.

We say yes to new tasks, projects, and events for a multitude of reasons, few of which directly relate to pushing us closer to what truly lights us up.

In other words, we are busy—very busy—with all kinds of activities that never bring us the results we want deep inside.

We want better health, but we spend our time eating foods that make us fat and avoiding activities that challenge our muscles.

We want a fulfilling career, but we settle for the employer that hired us and the boss that makes us miserable.

We want a purpose-driven life, but we gave up on that dream decades ago.

Free time is nice, but it is not the goal—it never was.

Purpose, passion, and an authentic zest for everyday life is so much more meaningful.

I do not claim to have all the answers, but I am certain of one thing: if we are to reach a point of true contentment with our lives, it will not show up in mundane activities that distract us from our most important work.

Our busyness is an epidemic, and letting go of just about everything is the cure.

STEP IV: CUT THE NONSENSE

Now that you have evaluated your life and work in this season, and clarified your vital few goals, it is time to systematically remove the obstacles standing between you and your simplified life.

The fourth step of *The Free-Time Formula* is to cut the nonsense, and it is divided into two parts: letting go and reducing friction.

In this chapter, we will walk through four strategies to help you identify what nonsense looks like in your world, and how you can expeditiously eradicate it.

In the next chapter, we will look at a variety of methods to improve your efficiency, so you can finish your work faster and with greater ease.

Let Go

1. Identify the Nonsense
2. Adopt Minimalism
3. Reject Perfectionism
4. Purge Your Commitments
5. Ring the Nonsense Alarm!

Reducing Friction

1. Procrastinating Intelligently
2. Eradicating Bad Habits
3. Passing the Baton

1. Identify the nonsense

I put twelve projects on hold to write this book.

I have dozens of ideas to build my business and have an impact on more people through a wide variety of pursuits: video courses, merchandise, high-end coaching services, hiring and training new employees, and many more.

When I began the writing process, I had to get clear on what mattered and what could be classified as pure distractions to my main objective: crafting an inspiring, actionable, and transformative book just for you.

Writing a book that meets my high bar is tough all by itself.

Writing a stellar book while also trying to juggle an incredible amount of other work is next to impossible. I had to make cuts, and doing so required me to identify what I now call "nonsense."

Anything that is a distraction to your vital few goals is nonsense.

Anything that never has to get done is nonsense.

Anything you would regret doing, or never regret not doing, is nonsense.

Anything that you know deep down is useless, silly, or ultimately not the highest and best use of your time is nonsense.

We need to find and eradicate the nonsense in your life, right now. To be clear, nonsense is subjective, so you will need to make these cuts on your own. However, once you know what matters, the rest should make itself known right away.

Begin by reviewing your vital few goals, and then analyze what else is true about your current circumstances.

- What is so important today that you should clear your calendar just to work on it?
- What tasks did you complete yesterday that you already know were a waste of your time?
- What projects have you committed to out of habit, convenience, loyalty, or obligation?

- What do you routinely do that only brings about mediocre results?
- What do you commonly regret doing?
- What tasks could be completed faster, more efficiently, or in batches to save precious time?
- What do you intuitively know about your schedule that needs to be corrected immediately?
- What have you said yes to that now needs a retraction?
- How much time could you free up if you simply cut the fruitless activity that consistently eats away at your calendar?

Acknowledging that you already waste time is a great first step. Directly responding to that waste by minimizing or eliminating it is brilliant, powerful, and the next most effective move you could make.

2. Adopt minimalism

Owning less is a critical step in the process to free up time, and an adoption of minimalism may be the most efficient way to dump what you do not need.

Minimalism can mean owning a tiny number of material possessions, but that is a narrow perspective and one that misses the boat on what it truly means to live with less.

Joshua Fields Millburn and Ryan Nicodemus, known as The Minimalists, define minimalism as *"a tool to rid yourself of life's excess in favor of focusing on what's important—so you can find happiness, fulfillment, and freedom"* (Millburn and Nicodemus, 2017).

According to Joshua Becker, author of the popular book on minimalism, *The More of Less: Finding the Life You Want under Everything You Own,* there are many incredible benefits to letting go of your excess stuff (Becker 2016, 8).

- More time and energy
- More money
- More generosity
- More freedom
- Less stress
- Less distraction
- Less environmental impact
- Higher-quality belongings
- A better example for our kids
- Less work for someone else
- Less comparison
- More contentment

And, even if the idea of minimalism inherently sounds too restricting, I highly recommend Greg McKeown's *Essentialism* approach, *"the relentless pursuit of less but better"* (McKeown 2014, 5).

Either way, adopting the principles behind minimalism can lead directly to the removal of physical stuff, as well as tasks, projects, events, and commitments from your calendar to free up enough tangible and intangible space in your life.

Due to my adoption of minimalism, I chose to make quite a few changes over the last few years:

1. Gave away half my wardrobe.
I realized that I only consistently wore about 30 percent of the clothes I owned, so I donated the vast majority of the remaining unworn items. I freed up space in my closet and learned to value the remaining clothing so much more.

2. Eliminated the use of paper.

By itself, paper can consume an office. When I switched to a digital-only system, I found that I regained an enormous amount of space and improved my productivity at the same time.

3. Chose a location for everything I owned.

Everything belongs somewhere, and once I embraced that mantra, I found a permanent home for all of my possessions. Sometimes that home was the trash or recycle bins, and sometimes I kept things in storage. Once I knew where it belonged, it went there and stayed there.

Getting rid of junk is revolutionary, whether it be superfluous material goods or excess body fat. The process of reorganizing each area of your life will clear your mind and calm your nerves.

Minimalism is freeing. It will bring clarity to your day that you otherwise would never experience.

Now, it's your turn.

Plan a day to purge your stuff. It will lighten your burdens and free your soul, I promise.

3. Reject perfectionism

Nashville is a beautiful town, and after six years in our apartment, my wife, Tessa, and I decided it was time to plant some roots.

We bought a great property outside the city near some cows and a river. The neighborhood is nice, and our neighbors are great people.

But (there's always a but), the previous owners of our house did next to nothing with the landscaping, leaving us with quite a bit of work. I had very little knowledge or experience in taking care of a yard, aside from mowing the grass as a kid.

The kicker is that our neighbor directly across the street is a professional landscaper.

Talk about keeping up with the Joneses!

I now needed to learn how to take care of my yard at a level I was not prepared for. In the first season, I did the bare minimum, simply ensuring the house would not become overrun with weeds and moles.

In the second season, I went all in, spending hundreds of hours mowing, trimming, sweeping, mulching, planting, weeding, digging, sweating, and learning more than I expected about half-moon edgers and electric versus gas-powered multifunction yard tools.

Today, my lawn is nice. I am proud of the work I did and the work I continue to do to keep everything looking beautiful.

However, there is one major problem with this scenario: *my yard does not have to look beautiful.*

Keeping my grass cut short is not one of my vital few goals. The status of our shrubbery or the height of our roses bushes has nothing to do with my long-term vision for a better life.

I created and solved a problem that never existed. No one told me the yard was a mess when I moved in—I made that up!

My perfectionism told me that I needed to make my yard look as good as my neighbor's—you know, the guy who designs professional landscaping blueprints for a living.

What I needed then, and what you may need now, is a "Good Enough" policy.

Most things in life will have to abide by this policy, or you will drive yourself mad. Most projects, tasks, priorities, and expectations will reach a point of good enough, and then *you must stop.*

Any effort exerted past good enough is wasted effort.

Perfectionism will tell you to keep going. It will demand you design a yard more jaw-dropping than the pro across the street.

Perfectionism will keep you up late at night, slaving away at a project that never has to be finished. That is not how you will free up time or accomplish your grandest goals.

Holding every idea, task, and project to a high bar is not only impossible, but it is also a recipe for burnout on every level. You will not make it.

The solution is simple, but challenging if you expect the best from yourself: you have to let go.

Let it go.

Let all of it go.

Turn on the *Frozen* soundtrack again. Buy the CD and play it in your car (if cars still have CD players).

Perfectionism, 4.0 GPAs, and being better than everyone around you at everything will not lead to a better life or the free time you are looking for.

Instead, it will burden you more than the real problems you need to solve and hold you back from accomplishing the vital few goals you are trying to finish.

Reject perfectionism, accept good enough, and center your greatest talents on the ambitious pursuits that will truly transform how you live.

4. Purge your commitments

The most direct method to cut nonsense and create free time on your calendar is to purge your current commitments in all areas of your life.

If you have not yet opened your calendar or to-do list to delete, postpone, cancel, and eliminate anything you can, this is your moment.

I go through a formal Weekly Review process (which you can read more about in my first book, *The 5 AM Miracle*) to thoroughly vet my calendar on a routine basis.

My review process includes a vitally important step of looking forward to the next week and clearing whatever I can to make room for my top three weekly goals.

Depending on the level of your attachment to the scheduled tasks, projects, and events already booked on your calendar, and your willingness (or lack thereof) to let someone down, this process could be your greatest challenge so far.

To help expedite the purge, follow a few simple steps:

1. Cut the easy stuff first, focusing on activities and events you could easily skip forever.
2. Cut tasks that you like but secretly know do not truly help in your quest to accomplish your vital few goals.
3. Evaluate the remaining items on your calendar to determine how closely they align with your current and most important objectives.
4. Upset one person. Go ahead and rip off the Band-Aid now because this is going to become part of your daily life. Tell one person you cannot attend their meeting, party, or conference call. Trust me; you will feel free and liberated when it is over.

Purging your commitments is not a single event—it is a lifestyle.

Saying no to others and yourself is about to become second nature, and it may be the one skill that sets you apart from your old self (and everyone else) faster than anything.

Later in the book, we will cover the specifics around cutting distractions from yourself and others. For now, keep your eye on the prize: eliminating absolutely everything you can from your calendar, task list, project list, personal responsibility list, or any other list you keep that tells you to do stuff.

No more doing—it is time for letting go.

The best action, in this case, is inaction. The more you eliminate, the more freedom you will have, instantly.

If you get good at this, and I hope you do, you may find a new favorite pastime in simply abolishing accumulated nonsense in all nooks and crannies of your life and work.

5. Ring the nonsense alarm!

Like gutters in a bowling alley, you will need clear indicators to alert when you are off track.

Spending time on unimportant tasks is common, and it happens to all of us in one form or another. However, this is a slippery slope.

How much nonsense is too much?

How can you clearly know when your schedule has gotten out of hand versus when you are doing well for this season?

The key is to create your beacon lights, your nonsense alarm system that will alert you to a productivity emergency.

CREATE YOUR MUST-DO LIST

Begin by creating your Must-Do List, a simple index of items near and dear to your heart, tasks that you are fully committed to accomplishing every week.

Then, at some point down the road, there will be a busy week and a hectic schedule. Some, or many, of the goals on your

Must-Do List will be sidelined and left undone. Though you have committed to a few key objectives, some will not get done.

This is your sign.

The alarm bells are now ringing. *You are too busy.*

If you have gone through the letting-go process outlined in this chapter and are still finding yourself too preoccupied for the few items on your Must-Do List, your life may be more off course than you realize.

This is your wake-up call.

When your Must-Do List is not getting done, this is a warning that you need to make a change, and it needs to happen right away. Continuing at the current pace will lead to increased stress, fatigue, mood swings, and burnout.

Build your beacons. Clarify your priorities. Know what must be accomplished to keep you at your best, and when those few things are threatened, you know what to do.

QUICK REVIEW: *LET IT GO*

1. Our busyness is an epidemic.

Free time is nice, but it is not the goal—it never was. Purpose, passion, and an authentic zest for everyday life is so much more meaningful. If we are to reach a point of true contentment with our lives, it will not show up in mundane activities that distract us from our most important work. Our busyness is an epidemic, and letting go of just about everything is the cure.

2. Know nonsense when you see it.

Anything that is a distraction from your vital few goals is nonsense. Anything that never has to get done is nonsense. Anything you would regret doing, or never regret not doing, is nonsense. Anything that you know deep down is useless, silly, or ultimately not the highest and best use of your time is nonsense.

3. **This is your moment.**
The most direct method to cut nonsense and create free time on your calendar is to purge your current commitments in all areas of your life. If you have not yet opened your calendar or to-do list to delete, postpone, cancel, and eliminate anything you can, the time is now.

CHAPTER 7 ACTION PLAN

1. **Identify the nonsense in your life and work.**
Ideally, anything that is not part of your vital few goals (potential nonsense) should be minimized or eliminated completely. Once you know what matters, everything else needs to go.

2. **Let go of your clutter and any excess junk that is holding you back.**
You may not be a hoarder, but the physical stuff in your life can act as a barrier to your progress. Adopt a healthy form of minimalism, reduce your footprint, and just let go.

3. **Purge your calendar, to-do list, and current commitments.**
Take time out of each week to thoroughly review what has landed on your calendar—and then cut whatever you can. Take time out to do the same process for your to-do list, project list, and any other optional activity that does not serve your vital few goals.

8

Reducing Friction

Minimizing Wasted Effort

I frequently take long road trips to and from Nashville, and I often find myself critiquing highway infrastructure—specifically, the shocking difference when you cross a state line.

If you find yourself heading east on Interstate 24 in southwestern Kentucky, you will eventually cross over into Tennessee. I love this distinct area because the portion of the road in Kentucky is a bumpy mess.

Initially, you may not necessarily notice the dilapidated condition of the road were it not for the dramatic difference just a few miles away.

As soon as you cross into Tennessee on your way toward Nashville, the sun is a little brighter, the trees lining the road are a little greener, and the road is miraculously smoother.

Every vehicle begins to drive faster, the friction on the road disappears, and you are greeted with a large "Welcome to Tennessee" sign that directs to you a beautiful visitor's center.

The rest of the drive into the city is amazing. It is fast, clean, and highly efficient, and I am sure I would not appreciate this specific section of road were it not for the pervasive bumps, potholes, and missing paint on the Kentucky side (*sorry, Kentucky*).

The clear difference between one state's highway maintenance and another's is the difference between a rough ride and smooth sailing—between dodging bullets and stepping on the gas—between obnoxious friction and beautiful harmony.

Friction is slowing you down.

Bumps in the road are delaying your progress and positioning obstacles between you and your vital few goals. Reducing or eliminating friction in your life and work is essential to cutting nonsense and accomplishing your goals faster.

When you minimize the amount of time spent on things that need to happen, remove excess bloat from your calendar, and smooth the path between point A and point B, you give yourself the best chance to free up time, reduce stress, and maximize your results.

PROCRASTINATING INTELLIGENTLY

In the previous chapter, you identified and removed unnecessary tasks, projects, events, and distractions from your calendar.

Now, with the remaining tasks on your plate, there are a variety of ways to arrange the puzzle of your calendar to get your most important work done. One highly effective method (which you will likely fall in love with right away) is intentionally procrastinating.

That's right!

You have my permission to put off your work—but there is an effective way to pull this off without finding yourself missing deadlines or dropping projects altogether.

What it means to procrastinate intelligently

Our goal is to reduce friction by scheduling must-do tasks at the exact right time. Using the pressure of looming deadlines, you can intelligently procrastinate when it serves you best.

Some tasks have no specific deadline, and therefore can be accomplished whenever you have a free minute (or eliminated if they are not important enough to be scheduled).

Other tasks absolutely must be accomplished by a strict cutoff time, in which case your calendar will have to align to those deadlines in a way that both completes the task on time and provides you the creative capacity to maximize the quality of your work.

For example, if my publisher told me I had twenty years to write this book, I may have postponed the work and taken the full twenty. However, I had six months, and that was an ideal time frame to accomplish the task, stay focused with a deadline, and hit my quality bar.

How procrastinating can reduce friction

Elaborating on this hypothetical twenty-year deadline, if I decided to spend two full decades working on this book I would inevitably do one of two things:

1. Wait until the very last minute to begin, in which case the deadline should never have been set so far in the future.
2. Spend considerably more time than I would need to finish the work and get the result I was seeking.

Deadlines need to be set in such a way that we can procrastinate just enough to complete the work on time without feeling extraordinary pressure (which could cause undue stress and a drop in quality) or endlessly expanding our work to fit the excessive time we were allowed, which is also known as Parkinson's Law (BusinessDictionary, 2017).

When you set appropriate time boundaries for your work, you can avoid waiting until the last minute and, simultaneously, not spend any more precious time than you would need.

It is more of an art than a science, but we are seeking to achieve our minimum viable effort, exerting no more than is necessary to get exactly what we intended.

This requires a bit of guesswork, experimentation, and a willingness to fail a few times. However, as you improve your self-awareness and find your rhythm with scheduling your work, you can dramatically reduce the amount of time you spend on any given task and maintain or improve the final product.

Also, though I was given six months to write this book, I wrote the whole thing from start to finish in less than three.

As much as I believe that I hate being pressured to do anything, nothing causes me to focus more in the moment and execute more effectively than an important and urgent deadline.

Pressure is the ultimate motivation for important work. When you have a strong reason to do something, you are compelled to act.

And as surprising as it may be, you do not need as much time as you think. You can do more with less, and a pressing deadline can be your best friend.

Filtering real work from bogus emergencies

There is nothing worse in the world of productivity than prioritizing work that never had to get done in the first place. You will get the satisfaction of checking off a box on your to-do list while going nowhere.

You are effectively treading water, spinning in circles, running on a hamster wheel, or _____ (insert your favorite metaphor for wasting your time here).

Real work deserves your attention. Urgent but meaningless distractions deserve the delete key.

Every office is a minefield. In the process of scheduling important work at just the right time, be on the lookout for misleading tangents and dangerous rabbit holes that will throw you off course, significantly delaying your progress.

As Stephen Covey taught in The *7 Habits of Highly Effective People*, we have to filter the urgent and unimportant (frequent distractions) from the truly urgent and important (real priorities). Very few things need to get done, while most need to be ignored, and it is your job to figure out which is which (Covey 2013, 160).

When you have a clear priority—an important and urgent task—you can effectively schedule it, leverage a healthy dose of pressure, and intelligently procrastinate as it best serves you.

ERADICATING BAD HABITS

Tiny decisions are the most treacherous.

It is the little things we do, or start to do, that grow over time, pick up speed, and escape our control. The tiny decisions become runaway trains, and our innocent choices blossom into bad habits.

We only meant to act upon these choices once or twice, but over time, and without warning, we discover those bad habits have grown into tiny villains and, eventually, colossal monsters.

For this book, a bad habit is any repeated behavior that impedes your ability to make direct progress on your vital few goals.

Anything you do over and over again that prevents you from spending precious time on what matters most is a bad habit, and it needs to be eradicated.

Essentially, bad habits are emotional addictions to activities with a low ROI.

The initial hit of dopamine and euphoria is enticing, but over time the high fades, leaving us only with the addiction of chasing what we once had.

Vegging on the couch is great after a long run or a hard week at the office. Lounging on the sofa for five hours a day, every day, is no longer fun or sexy—it is a direct barrier to your health and your future.

- What do you repeatedly act upon that you already know is not working for you?
- How do you normally respond when life is getting difficult? Do you have any vices that you lean on to ease the stress?
- Have you caught yourself in a downward spiral, doing an activity over and over again, but without any tangible results to show for it?

This may be the most difficult part of habit change: acknowledging that you are drowning because of choices you have made. You committed to too many things, started too many bad habits, and said yes to too many activities that were destined to throw you off course.

The good news is that you can change. You have the power to "un-commit," to right the ship, to eradicate a bad habit and become a new person.

Habit change is not an immediate process, but neither was forming the bad habit in the first place. Long-term change takes a long time, but the time will pass anyway.

In a year, you will be a year older. The only question is: When you look back one year from now, will you have made better choices? Will you have changed? Will you have stopped the cycle?

PASSING THE BATON

Aside from eliminating a task entirely, delegating it to someone else may be the most direct method of removing it from your to-do list.

In sticking with our goal of reducing friction so that you can accomplish your vital few goals more effectively, passing off your work to another capable person is a sure-fire way to allow you to do what you do best.

One of the fundamental principles of time management often missed by overzealous high achievers is that you do not have to do everything yourself.

Let me say that one more time.

You do not have to do it all—and you should not even attempt to do so.

Passing the baton to someone else (or a machine through automation) is not a fancy privilege for managers who can assign work to their directs—it is a vital component for all of us to let go of everything that is not the highest and best use of our time.

Sometimes we have no choice and find ourselves completing tasks that someone else could and likely should be doing for us. As an entrepreneur, I can tell you firsthand that I wear many hats—*way too many hats*.

As an achiever, you too wear too many hats, and it is time you took some off.

If eliminating a task or project is not possible, consider how you can off-load your work in the most effective manner.

1. Delegate it.

If you are in a position to directly pass off work to a direct report, and it is in the best interest of both you and the direct, go for it. Utilizing the strengths, talents, and availability of those who work for you is smart business, but it is also a tremendous gift and can free up some much-needed time.

2. Outsource it.

Hiring virtual assistants can be a simple and affordable solution to many problems. Over the years, I have outsourced more work than I believed was possible, and in many cases, I saved myself tremendous time, energy, and money.

3. Automate it.

Much of our work today can be handled more effectively with a well-built system than by our own two hands. If your task can be automated, invest the needed time today to free up tremendous time tomorrow.

4. Dump it.

If no one else can handle it, and you really should not be working on it, let it go. Delete the task and move on. I have surprised myself many times when I realize my "important" projects never have to be completed—ever.

A WORD OF CAUTION FOR CONTROL FREAKS

If you are anything like me, a self-identified control freak, letting go of vitally important work can be highly emotional. I never want someone else to do something that I know I could do better myself.

The problem is that this mindset is one of the direct causes of high stress, high blood pressure, long work hours, and burnout. *You cannot and should not do everything.*

Yes, I will continue to say this over and over again throughout the book because it is the message you (*cough—I—cough*) need to hear again and again.

Though it is possible that your work will not be done to your normal standards, letting someone else take the reins means you can spend your precious time on the vital few tasks that only you can do.

There are only a few tasks meant just for you, and it is your job to identify those tasks and spend as much time on them as possible.

The only way this is possible is if other people or systems take over everything else as much as possible.

QUICK REVIEW: REDUCING FRICTION

1. **Minimize wasted effort.**

   Friction is slowing you down. Bumps in the road are delaying your progress and positioning obstacles between you and your vital few goals. Reducing or eliminating friction in your life and work is essential to cutting nonsense and accomplishing your goals faster.

2. **Work just in time.**

   You can reduce friction by scheduling must-do tasks at the exact right time, neither too early nor too late. Using the pressure of looming deadlines, you can intelligently procrastinate when it serves you best to achieve your minimum viable effort, exerting no more than is necessary to get exactly what you intended.

3. You do not have to do it all yourself.

You should not even attempt to do so. Passing the baton to someone else (or a machine through automation) is not a fancy privilege for managers who can assign work to their directs—it is a vital component for all of us to let go of everything that is not the highest and best use of our time.

Chapter 8 Action Plan

1. Filter real work from bogus emergencies.

There is nothing worse in the world of productivity than prioritizing work that never had to get done in the first place. You will get the satisfaction of checking off a box on your to-do list while going nowhere. Real work deserves your attention. Delete and prevent all urgent but meaningless distractions.

2. Directly address your obstacles to scheduling your vital few goals.

We all have bad habits, old tendencies, prior commitments, and emotional attachments to the things we do on a regular basis. In all likelihood, your biggest obstacles are your habits, and the beliefs you hold about what is possible for you to achieve. Tackle your obstacles head-on.

3. Procrastinate intelligently.

Some work is best done at the last minute—not all work, but some. Carefully analyze the projects on your plate and determine what is best suited for working on just ahead of the deadline. This one strategy alone could dramatically reduce unnecessary waste and worry.

STEP

V

Schedule What Matters

9

Red-Carpet Calendar

Best Intentions

I gained thirty pounds (thirteen and a half kilos) during the first semester of my freshman year of college.

Yeah, I did that.

My transition from high school to college was more than an opportunity to move out of my parents' house and into a dorm—it was also the first time in my life that I had full control over my calendar.

I shifted from scheduling my entire life inside a paper planner to using what I believed was the future of personal tech, a Palm Pilot. Remember those?

I shifted from following a preset schedule to creating my own. I had real power over my life for the first time, and I had no idea what to do with it.

My first inclination was to schedule my classes, book a few sessions at the university's gym, and leave plenty of open space for social time.

So far, so good.

Then, on the very first day of class, I popped by the cafeteria for a quick bite. I was surprised at the enormous selection of food, so I ate a full breakfast, went to class, and returned a few hours later for lunch.

What I saw next surprised me even more.

Some of the same people I saw at breakfast were still in the cafeteria. They had never left. They were still eating....

What?!

Then it hit me: my new cafeteria allowed you to eat as much as you wanted for every meal. There was no limit if you stayed.

Boom!

That was it. I was hooked. I began eating gargantuan-sized meals. I ate whatever I could get my hands on and then went back for more.

Combine my new obsession for eating with my frequent social outings, and you can imagine what I was doing to my body in short order.

Calendar? What calendar? I had new priorities now.

Three months and thirty pounds later, I returned home for the holiday break, and my family's collective jaw fell on the floor. *Who was this guy? This is not the Jeff Sanders we dropped off in the fall.*

I had made a few (or more) rather poor decisions, and it was written all over my chunky face.

I had scheduled what mattered to me: eating and drinking as much as possible. I prioritized classes and studying just enough, but I made plenty of room for what I wanted most.

My calendar never showed how much time I was spending at meals and parties. If you only knew me through what I booked on my calendar, you would believe I was a solid student who attended classes, studied, worked out, and was involved in plenty of extracurricular activities.

This is what a calendar can become—a storage bin for your best intentions.

Ideally, a calendar is designed to closely represent what you are going to do, not just visualize a fantasy that you rarely review.

If the events on your calendar and your actual day-to-day choices are a major mismatch, it is time for an overhaul.

STEP V: SCHEDULE WHAT MATTERS

We have reached the stage of execution. This is your moment to take action and begin gaining real traction on your ambitious pursuits!

Now that you have evaluated where you are in this season of your life, clarified your vital few goals, and cut everything else, it is time for the next step.

The fifth step of *The Free-Time Formula* is to schedule what matters, and it is divided into two parts: creating your Red-Carpet Calendar and deciding what to do with all your free time!

Red-Carpet Calendar

1. Calendar Intervention
2. Create Your Red-Carpet Calendar
3. Batching and Theme Days
4. Ten Common Obstacles to Calendaring

What to Do with All That Free Time!

1. Three Planning Models of Free Time
2. Mindless

3. Mindful
4. Structured Spontaneity
5. Best Use of Your Free Time

CALENDAR INTERVENTION

Does your calendar need an intervention?

Do you frequently find yourself staring at your day's task list and wondering how any of this stuff will ever actually get done?

Do you miss big deadlines? Flake on important meetings? Or frequently show up late to appointments?

There are two major elements to calendars that cause problems like these and quickly result in failure: poor planning and poor execution.

Poor planning means that the layout of the calendar does not align with reality: time estimations are inaccurate, tasks are scheduled in the wrong order, important events are missing, or a multitude of other possibilities that cause the calendar to misrepresent how you live and work each day.

Poor execution simply means you did not do what you planned to do, though there is no good reason for it. In other words, you dropped the ball, procrastinated, got distracted, or just never felt compelled to do what you told yourself was critical to get done.

The bulk of this book is dedicated to helping you plan more effectively, to prevent missed deadlines and schedule your most important goals above all else.

If you struggle with poor execution, you will be pleased to know that you can solve the majority of those issues with better planning.

Overhauling your calendar is a great synonym for aligning your calendar to fit you better, and to fit how you want to operate each day.

Restructure your expectations

Though I firmly believe in self-discipline as a highly effective strategy for squeezing more value out of your time, often the best approach is to make your calendar adapt to your ideal lifestyle—not the other way around.

Your calendar intervention is a restructuring of your priorities, but more importantly, it is a restructuring of your expectations.

You are not your ideal self, and your calendar is never going to forecast your day perfectly.

Your ideal self and ideal schedule will always elude you. They are ghosts, mythical creatures that we are dying to believe in but secretly know will never manifest.

- If you expect too much from your calendar, your calendar will fail you.
- If you expect too much from others, they will fail you.
- If you expect too much from yourself, *you* will fail you.

The odds are that you will need a calendar intervention every week to align your expectations with your current reality—to remind you that you are only human and you can only do so much.

With your limitations and flawed expectations in mind, it is time to create a calendar that will let you shine in your best way possible.

CREATE YOUR RED-CARPET CALENDAR

A well-designed, properly prioritized calendar is a beautiful and rare beast.

It is not something I often see because what I often see is either a sparse collection of random events or an overprogrammed monstrosity that gives me an immediate headache.

In the context of *The Free-Time Formula*, a well-designed calendar is your red-carpet moment, a calendar that puts your best work and vital few goals in the spotlight and allows them to sparkle.

Think about your current calendar and determine how many of these elements of a Red-Carpet Calendar are true for you today:

- Priority-first booking (what matters most is scheduled first)
- Plenty of margin for surprise tasks, unexpected challenges, and down time
- Synchronization across devices and between applications (calendar is available everywhere you go and syncs up with other tools you use)
- Easy to adjust and modify tasks (date, times, descriptions)
- Easy to share with others (making collaboration and group work a breeze)
- Similar tasks booked in batches (eliminating friction of task switching)
- Theme days assigned to major projects (reducing additional friction of project switching)

This list is not comprehensive, though these are core elements that most great calendars possess. Try not to get hung up on the technology side. We will discuss that element soon.

The key is to ensure that what matters most gets scheduled, and what gets scheduled gets done. The rest is a matter of personal preference, adjusting to company expectations, and adapting your calendar to your current season.

Converting your current calendar into a Red-Carpet Calendar can be as simple as tweaking a few scheduled tasks, or as complex as starting from scratch and rebuilding everything from the ground up.

In my experience, starting from scratch, though it sounds like significantly more work, is often the fastest and most effective means of getting the result you want—assuming your calendar is a mess and needs some serious work.

To help with the rebuilding process, take advantage of the beauty and simplicity of batching and theme days.

BATCHING AND THEME DAYS

Inefficiencies run rampant in every office and on every calendar, and most of your wasted time can be prevented with simple changes in how your time gets booked.

Two of the greatest strategies I have utilized myself, and taught my clients, are batching and theme days.

These two strategies alone can save you a dozen hours or more every week. I can personally attest to the power of these methods as I used both of them to write this book in a shockingly short period of time.

Here is the process at a glance to optimize your calendar and reduce friction through effective weekly planning:

1. Clarify your vital few goals for the week.
2. Assign themes to the next seven to fourteen days.
3. Schedule batching sessions for similar tasks.

We covered clarifying your vital few goals in chapter 3, so once you have those set, you can begin to effectively plan your next week or two with appropriate themes.

Assign themes to the next 7–14 days

The concept behind a theme day is that you work on one major project each day. The theme of the day dictates what gets scheduled and, inherently, what does not.

I have hosted a weekly podcast for years and usually need to spend one full workday developing each episode. Mondays are my podcasting days, so my goal is to ensure I only schedule podcast-related tasks on Mondays.

This also means I try not to schedule any podcast-related tasks on any other day of the week.

This ensures I can focus exclusively on one project for the day, which boosts my productivity, allows for connections between tasks I otherwise might have missed, and ensures I always have the time I need for that vital goal. Here is an example schedule with theme days:

- Monday = Podcasting
- Tuesday = Marketing
- Wednesday = Grad School Projects
- Thursday = Admin Tasks
- Friday = Meetings
- Saturday = Self-Care & Exercise
- Sunday = Family Time

This example is based on my calendar as an entrepreneur, which means I usually have the flexibility to set my schedule. If your calendar is pre-set by an employer, boss, or anyone else, consider when you could apply a theme day inside your normally working hours, or even at home.

For example, it is quite easy to assign themes for your household chores.

- Monday = Recycling
- Tuesday = Trash
- Wednesday = Laundry
- Thursday = Wash Cars
- Friday = Pay Bills
- Saturday = Full House Cleaning
- Sunday = Yard Work

The goal is to optimize the value of themes whenever and wherever you can. This not only allows for easier scheduling, but you will certainly get more done and reduce your stress when everything has a proper place on your calendar.

Schedule batching sessions for similar tasks

Batching can be utilized in conjunction with theme days, or by itself.

The key to batching is to schedule similar tasks in one block of time. This may be the best way to schedule what matters, reduce friction on a daily basis, and improve focus for any project.

When you batch similar projects together, you can give yourself fully to the work at hand and find efficient ways to move faster from one task to the next.

As a counter example, if you had to seal and mail a hundred letters, it would be highly inefficient to mail one letter per day. The best method would be to set up a work table for sealing, labeling, and stamping each letter in an assembly-line style.

This would reduce setup time, takedown time, and all of the tiny spaces of time between each specific step. When you add together the tiny spaces each day, you can find hours of time you previously had lost.

Batching improves efficiency, reduces time-wasting activities between tasks (bathroom breaks, chatting with coworkers, checking email, and so forth), and leads to higher quality and quantity of work produced.

Over the last few years I have learned a few key lessons from implementing both batching and theme days:

1. **It is best to focus on one thing at a time.**

   With only one day to work on a project, or set of similar tasks, you have to focus because the clock is ticking. You only have today, so slacking off is not an option.

2. **You have the freedom to dive deep.**

   You can give yourself the freedom to take the time you need for important projects. You can get more done on a single project if you give yourself the breadth to work on it all day—without trying to squeeze in time for other unrelated tasks and projects (which ultimately just become distractions).

3. **It is easier to schedule tasks.**

   When a new idea pops up, set it aside to dive into it on its dedicated theme day. This prevents distraction from working on other projects ahead of time when something more pressing needs your attention now.

4. **You will feel more accomplished.**

   You feel better when you do something big than when you attempt a thousand tiny and unrelated tasks. Focusing on a single important goal each day always leads to more progress, fulfillment, and the desire to repeat that process again and again.

TEN COMMON OBSTACLES TO CALENDARING

1. I don't control my calendar

There are many professions where your daily schedule is pre-set by your employer, or by factors well beyond your control. Teachers are great examples of this scenario.

If your calendar is predetermined, work with what you have. There is always more flexibility built in than you see at first glance.

Often the best approach is to seek out the most productive people at your company and figure out what they are doing that appears to help them get more done than anyone else. Copy their methods. Steal their ideas.

You do not have to reinvent the wheel to optimize your daily schedule.

2. I don't know which important task to accomplish next—everything is a priority!

There is only one priority at any given time. Though you will certainly encounter situations where many tasks are important, only one deserves your undivided attention.

Also, and this will be a little painful, you may have to let some goals go. You may have to miss a deadline, skip a meeting, or let someone down. Often the best approach to adhering to your top priority is to acknowledge the consequences of doing so.

If you plan ahead and communicate effectively with others involved in your work, you may be surprised to find that you can bump a task, postpone a project, or get a little leeway on your looming deadline.

3. Which digital calendar is best? Google Calendar, Apple Calendar, Microsoft Outlook...?

The specific calendar you choose is likely the least important element in helping you rein in the chaos of your daily schedule.

HOW you use the calendar is everything. WHICH calendar you use is a matter of personal preference.

As a reminder, these elements are very helpful when considering a digital solution:

- Synchronization across devices and between applications (calendar is available everywhere you go and syncs up with other tools you use)
- Easy to adjust and modify tasks (date, times, descriptions)
- Easy to share with others (making collaboration and group-work a breeze)

4. I can't commit to any specific calendar, or I use too many

Consolidation is your best friend. The fewer tools you use, the better.

If it is possible to use your work calendar to schedule all of your personal tasks as well, do so. One calendar is cleaner and simpler than two.

If you find yourself stretched across a half dozen apps, programs, and planners you will certainly only add to the stress and complication of figuring out the next best move.

In the end, simplicity always wins.

5. I procrastinate and can't get started

As we discussed in chapter 8, there are effective ways to procrastinate intelligently. However, if you still find it increasingly difficult to break through the wall of inertia and just begin, try a few of these strategies:

Pick something easy and go!
Building momentum is the key to killing procrastination. Choose a task that is super easy, so easy you cannot imagine *not* doing it. Let that one tiny action flow into subsequent large and more impactful actions.

Guarantee you cannot fail.
Put yourself in a situation where the only logical next action is forward progress. For example, have a friend drop you off 26.2 miles from your house, forcing you to run the full marathon distance back home.

Create a 100 percent distraction-free environment.
When you block yourself from every possible activity besides the one you have to do, the work magically gets done.

Practice self-discipline.
Nothing works better than building your discipline muscles, so that you have the power to overcome any obstacle that comes your way. As often as possible, put yourself in situations where you have to fight against the forces of distraction to achieve your goal.

6. I don't have the self-discipline to follow through on my plan

If self-discipline is not an effective means just yet, lean on others to push you across the finish line. Accountability is the most effective strategy for most people because outside influence is powerful. We do not want to let others down, and we care about our image.

Create your own Calendar Board of Advisers, a group of people who hold you to your plan of action for specific goals. This could include your boss for work tasks, a spouse or partner for household projects, or a personal trainer for health and fitness goals.

7. I don't have the energy to do what I want

Energy is an assumed element in the world of productivity. In other words, it may be the most overlooked characteristic of your daily plan.

If you do not have the energy to follow through on your goal, you will either not get it done, or consistently rely on stimulants to push you through. Neither of these is ideal.

If a lack of energy is a recurring issue for you, then your health is now one of your vital few goals. Without your health and energy to execute on your goals, you will have no goals.

If you are too tired to do what matters, nothing matters.

8. I don't understand the technology, so I opt for old-school paper even though I know it's not as efficient

Paper planners are great. Though I switched to a paperless system and will likely never go back, I effectively used a paper planner for years, and it got the job done.

In many scenarios, paper is preferred over digital because it will not distract you. Paper planners will not alert you to a new Facebook post or ping you to read that latest email.

Before you feel guilty about not using the latest gadgets, take a minute to realize the true value of what you are already using.

9. I can't accurately estimate the length of my tasks

No one is good at this. Trust me. The only tasks that can be accurately estimated are those you have done hundreds of times already and for which you can easily determine exactly what has to be achieved.

However, improving your estimation skills is critical if you want to effectively schedule what matters. The best way to do this is with boundaries.

Nothing is more effective at ending a task than a firm boundary. Deadlines work. Timers work. Accountability works.

Use whatever you have available to end a task on a specific date and time, ensuring that you will finish the job before it is due.

10. My calendar is a lost cause, so I gave up on it and just wing it every day

I once spoke with a woman at a conference who gave up on email. She had over 107,000 unread messages on her phone and gave me more excuses for why email was worthless than I have ever heard.

She gave up on email—email did not give up on her.

Your calendar is not a lost cause. It can and should be saved. The key is to believe in its potential to assist you in accomplishing what matters most in your life.

If you have to start over, start over. If you have to delete everything, rebuild a whole new plan, and mess up your life in the short term, so be it. Making the most of your life means optimizing the precious hours you have on earth.

Do not let the obstacles of learning new technology or asking tough questions about your priorities stop you from becoming your best self.

QUICK REVIEW: *RED-CARPET CALENDAR*

1. **Your calendar should not become a storage bin for your best intentions.**

   Red-Carpet Calendars accurately represent how you live and work on most days. Well-designed calendars shine a light on your vital few goals and give you the margin to rest when you need it. If your calendar is not aligned to you, turn the tables around and make the necessary adjustments.

2. **Batching and Theme Days can save you a dozen hours or more every week.**

   When you combine like items together, you can remove incredible amounts of time normally allocated for switching back and forth between unrelated projects. Scheduling your vital few goals in batches can also ensure that you make tremendous progress, connect ideas you may have missed, and provide a serious sense of accomplishment.

3. **Your calendar is not a lost cause.**

   It can and should be optimized to give you the best chance to become your best self. If your calendar is out of control, rein it in. If it is messy, clean it up. If you do not see the light at the end of the tunnel, clear the tunnel and start over. Your calendar is meant to assist you in accomplishing your vital few goals, and if it is not doing that, it is time for an intervention.

CHAPTER 9 ACTION PLAN

1. **Create your Red-Carpet Calendar.**

   To make consistent progress on your vital few goals, it will be essential for you to schedule what matters most, first. Your Red-Carpet Calendar is your ticket to making space for your highest-value activities, those few projects that will create the biggest impact, while continually eliminating everything that stands in your way.

2. **Assign Theme Days to your calendar and batch similar work together.**

One of the fastest ways to increase your efficiency is to do one thing at a time. Whenever possible, schedule like items together. Find creative ways to batch your work, and you will see an immediate boost in your ability to get things done.

3. **Optimize your calendaring tools.**

Your tools are meant to assist you, not become an obstacle themselves. Most often I see people who struggle to make the most out of the tools they already have, meaning that right now you have access to everything you need to move forward. Take advantage of what you have access to and make the most of it.

10

What to Do with All That Free Time

Free Time Is Not Netflix Time

I once interviewed a great personal trainer named Ted Ryce, host of *The Legendary Life Podcast*, who told me, "Soreness is not progress—progress is progress" (Ryce, 2015).

Well, free time is not Netflix time—Netflix time is Netflix time.

Your time off the clock is your time. You can do whatever you want with it, but commonly we spend that time doing what we have always done—without a second thought, and without regarding any sense of boundaries for the activities we have mindlessly chosen.

In the process of writing this book, I hit a wall, a mental block, and was ready for a good break. I went to Facebook and asked for recommendations for a great television series to dig into during my own free time.

Within minutes I had dozens of responses. Not at all surprising to me was that nearly everyone recommended I watch every season of *Breaking Bad* immediately!

Entertaining our brains with media is the norm. If you asked connected people for recommendations, you would get hundreds or thousands of ideas—more entertainment than you will ever have time to consume in ten lifetimes.

We are connected. We are distracted. We are conditioned to spend our time off the clock in pursuit of the next dopamine hit.

What we often do, myself included, is fall into bad habits and mental ruts because it is the easiest choice, the path of least resistance.

We commute home after a long day at the office, pour a glass of wine, and start watching a random show.

Weeks go by, and the habits continue. Another long day, another glass of wine, more random nonsense.

Months go by, and the habits get worse. Another long day, two glasses of wine, three hours of useless, life-numbing entertainment.

Years go by, and we are stuck for good. Another long day, still drinking, still watching, still not making progress on anything of value.

The problem here is not alcohol, entertainment, or your current vice. The problem is not relaxing, taking a break, or vegging out after working hard.

The problem is the mindless behavior, the little treats we give ourselves that evolve into little monsters.

The problem is our free time no longer feels like free time, or we believe we have no free time at all because all of our actual free time has already been claimed years ago by routine behavior.

We have a choice when it comes to our free time.

We can spend our time progressively working toward results we truly and enthusiastically care about, or we can numb out, disappear, and dissociate with the real power we have over our activities.

If you want the make the most of *The Free-Time Formula*, this is it. This is where you can not only carve out the time you want but get the beautiful benefits you have been dreaming about.

THREE PLANNING MODELS OF FREE TIME

I like to plan things, most things. Well . . . just about everything.

I tend to obsessively plan my life and prefer it that way. Not everything in your life needs a plan, but it is possible and wise to effectively plan both proactively and reactively.

You can dictate much of your life before it happens on paper, or preempt your impulsivity in such a way that you can avoid wasting large amounts of time due to bad habits and decision fatigue.

When it comes to free time, there are three planning models we instinctively follow that habitually dictate our behavior: mindless, mindful, and structured spontaneity.

In other words, you will do what you always do, what you planned to do, or what makes the most sense based on what you would love to do.

Whether you realize it or not, this is what you do whenever free time shows up. One of these three planning models is your go-to, your innate pattern of conduct. If you believe your pattern is leading in the wrong direction, this is a good time to change.

1. MINDLESS

The most common planning model of free time lacks any plan at all.

What many of us tend to do is what we have always done. Maybe a plan was made months or years ago, but it has been abandoned and replaced by routine and pointless pursuits.

Your habits may not appear to be pointless, but are you proactively planning your free time? Are you getting the results you want from your time off the clock? Do you find yourself back on the couch, again, and cannot remember how you got there, *again*?

Mindless behavior is not all bad. Technically, great habits can become mindless, just as bad habits can. The clear difference lies in the results.

If habitually lounging around the house in your pajamas made you rich, that specific behavior would be instantly and repeatedly reinforced. Unfortunately, that is not the case (*if it is, call me!*), and we often lack the energy to choose to take off the PJs to do anything more productive.

We most often tend to find ourselves engaging in mindless behavior due to exhaustion and decision fatigue.

As the *New York Times* explains, "*The more choices you make throughout the day, the harder each one becomes for your brain, and eventually, it looks for shortcuts, usually in either of two very different ways. One shortcut is to become reckless: to act impulsively instead of expending the energy to first think through the consequences. (Sure, tweet that photo! What could go wrong?) The other shortcut is the ultimate energy saver: do nothing*" (Tierney, 2011).

When your free time results in reckless behavior or total stagnation, nothing productive is getting done. You have mindlessly trapped yourself in a vicious cycle of inaction, ultimately leading to falling behind, feeling worse about yourself, and failing to recover intelligently from the normal wear and tear of your work.

Mindless free time is wildly ineffective.

Lacking a productive plan for how to best optimize the precious free time you have is a ticking time bomb.

You will eventually find yourself engaging in destructive behavior because that is what we do—we take shortcuts, we become reckless, or we just sit on the couch.

Either way, we have squandered the opportunity . . . again.

I see mindless behavior like this rear its ugly head most often after a long, hard day, or when too much free time is on the calendar, or both.

Yes, there is such a thing as *too much* free time. That may sound like a fantasy, but it is real, and it negatively affects you more than you realize.

Imagine you just returned home after a difficult day at work. You decide to relax by watching the latest episode of your favorite show before heading off to bed. Somehow you end up watching four episodes, back to back to back to back, without so much as pausing to acknowledge the choice you just made.

Think about this common scenario. You left work believing you only had enough free time for a single episode, yet managed to watch four.

Yes! You have more free time than you think—you are simply spending that time on activities with a very low ROI, often without realizing the misstep until it is too late.

This is one of the most important lessons in the book, so please highlight and frame that last sentence.

What could have occurred in this scenario is that after watching the one episode you could have read a book, called a friend, or just gone to sleep early—all of which would have been a higher and better use of your time.

Maybe this binge-watching scenario does not fit your life exactly. But doesn't it?

Are there not times in your weekly schedule where you planned a short break but wound up taking a much longer and unnecessary one?

Are there not circumstances where you believed you had no time for yourself but ended up engaging in activities that never needed to happen at all?

We all fall victim to mindless behavior, so the question is not how can we eradicate it, but how can we minimize it?

How can we more proactively structure our time off, and guard ourselves against letting low-value activities balloon into massive time wasters?

How can we intelligently plan our time to consistently get productive, rejuvenating, and prosperous results from it?

2. MINDFUL

Mindful planning is proactive.

It is time on your calendar that is exclusively reserved for your vital few goals, or serious leisure activities that challenge you and cause you to grow.

It is nonnegotiable time that guarantees you will get what you need to stay happy, focused, and productive.

Mindful free time could occur in small blocks or large chunks, in tiny windows during your normal work day or all weekend long—either way, it consists of preplanned and intelligently chosen, high-value activities.

Training for a triathlon, learning to cross-stitch, taking a hardcore nap, or planning an international trip to explore the Amazon rainforest are all great examples of mindfully using your free time if (and this is a BIG if), those specific choices help you:

1. Make direct progress toward your vital few goals;
2. Help you become a higher and better version of yourself; and
3. Directly assist in your recovery so you can spend your on-the-clock time doing your best work.

That is the whole list. Ideally, all of your free time will be classified as falling into one or more of these elements.

Considering that free time can either be squandered or seized, the choice is obvious: mindless free time is out and mindful free time is in.

Double-edged sword of Type A people

A word of caution to the high achievers, overachievers, and those who obsessively work way too much: *mindful free time is not the same as working to the bone.*

I want to put a strong emphasis on the third element to directly assist in your recovery.

I love working as much as any passionate, Type A, go-getter out there. I have loved working so much that it has backfired in ways I could never have expected.

Proactively planning your life is a holistic pursuit—meaning your plans must consist of working and pausing, rhythmically digging in and systemically pulling back, purposefully choosing to engage fully and disengage fully.

When you plan your free time, pause before you commit to anything.

Spend an hour, a half day, or as much time as it takes to zero in on what rejuvenates your soul, what brings you back to life, and what can truly enhance the work you dearly love to do so much.

I need this message just as much as you do.

We all benefit when we mindfully step back, reflect, and dig in again feeling refreshed and ready for action!

3. STRUCTURED SPONTANEITY

The final free time planning model is the most flexible and has the greatest potential to help you live in the present moment.

Structured spontaneity is being proactively reactive—it is opportunistic time.

In a nutshell, it means that when free time appears, you are ready with an energetic curiosity and willingness to go with the flow.

- When space magically shows up on your calendar, you take advantage of it.
- When a meeting is unexpectedly canceled, you swoop in with a brilliant next move.
- When you discover you have no formal plans for the weekend, you review your list of amazing projects to work on and jump in feet first.

Type B people will thrive here.

Create your "free time? do this now" list

To take advantage of free time that shows up unexpectedly, be prepared with your *"Free Time? Do This Now"* list.

This is a collection of tasks, projects, or ideas, varying in length, that you could pursue when you discover an opening in your schedule.

- **Fifteen minutes available?** Meditate, practice yoga, or text a friend.
- **One hour available?** Read a book or knock out the next task on your current goal.
- **Half a day available?** Go on a long hike or catch up on projects that you have fallen behind on.
- **More than one day available?** Focus exclusively on the one project you have been neglecting and which would make you feel incredible to finally finish.

The key to this list is prepared impulsivity. In other words, you have a variety of ideas preplanned that you would love to work on, but rarely find the time for.

When the time pops up, and it will, you can take advantage of those opportunities and make the most of the time that would normally be wasted.

Change your default behavior

When free time appears on your calendar, change your default behavior to align with your pre-chosen, high-value activities.

Think of it as "this not that."

- Meditation, not Facebook
- Reading, not TV
- Water, not junk food
- Yoga, not needlessly worrying

Or "this before that."

- Water before coffee
- Planning before diving in
- Salad before dessert
- Exercise before going out
- Big goals before email
- Gratitude before criticism

Structure your time off

Planning your weekends will not take away from the beauty of living in the moment. It is a common belief that planning removes your ability to be creative, impulsive, or present.

It is just not true.

Planning gives you the structure and boundaries to thrive. Limiting yourself gives you more freedom, not less.

Setting up boundaries prevents you from wasting your free time on more of the same low-value activities that you always do.

Structure gives you direction, clarity, and a goal to focus on. Structure gives you a tangible plan to work with and a reason to get out of bed early on a Saturday morning.

Your time off needs structure more than you realize, much more.

Whether you are an over-the-top achiever or a fly-by-the-seat-of-your-pants person, you will benefit from more structure when you least expect it to help.

BEST USE OF YOUR FREE TIME

I often wonder what my life was like before social media and the Internet.

I wonder because sometimes it seems as though technology at the current level has existed forever, though I know that is not the case.

I grew up just as the Internet was going mainstream. During the tech boom of the late 1990s, I was a teenager. In my childhood years, I spent my free time playing sports and video games, while my teen years were consumed with figuring out how to check my AOL email very slowly on a dial-up connection.

How you use your free time matters a great deal. In fact, there is a stark difference between playing a physically active game with your friends and mindlessly floating from one website to another by yourself every weekend.

Katrina Onstad, author of *The Weekend Effect: The Life-Changing Benefits of Taking Time Off and Challenging the Cult of Overwork,* highlights that our leisure falls into the categories of casual or serious (Onstad, 2017).

While casual pursuits like online shopping or binge drinking provide immediate gratification, those activities are usually holistically shallow in the long run.

Serious leisure pursuits, such as diligently practicing the violin or researching weather patterns for your next backpacking trip, are far more beneficial and rewarding.

As Katrina Onstad states, *"The weekend goal should be 'eudaimonic' happiness, which is a sense of well-being that arises from meaningful, challenging activities that cause you to grow as a person. This means spending the weekend on serious leisure activities that require the regular refinement of skills"* (Onstad, You're doing your weekend wrong).

Every season of your life will provide new opportunities to make the most of the margins in your calendar, and the season you are in now is no different.

Now that you have clarified your vital few goals, cleared your calendar of extraneous nonsense, scheduled time for your ambitious pursuits, and have reviewed the three planning models of free time, consider these options for how to make the most of your current time off the clock.

1. Brain dump

Begin by making a list of everything you could pursue. Brainstorm ideas for all of the possible ways you could, and would ideally love to, optimize your free time.

Approach this exercise with a mindset focused on what you need and want most, not on what you have been doing thus far.

Remember, the goal is to proactively optimize the small windows of time you have available. That time could be spent mindlessly doing random things, or consciously making a dramatic difference.

2. Make progress on your vital few goals

I tend to use every minute of free time I can on the few goals I have set. This could lead to overkill and burnout quickly if you have already spent a large chunk of your week on these goals, so approach this strategy cautiously.

However, if one of your vital few goals is fitness or family related, for example, you may be able to dive into these areas with intensity during every minute you are not at the office.

I trained and ran a dozen marathons in a three-year stretch in my twenties using only my free time on nights and weekends. A lot can happen when you focus exclusively on one objective and put your whole self behind it.

3. Recover intelligently

Yes, sometimes Netflix is the best choice. Free time is not Netflix time—except when it is.

Recovering intelligently means choosing wisely to sleep, take naps, watch movies, read a book under a tree, lay out on the beach, get a massage, or spend an hour in an isolation tank.

Whatever you need, do it. Whatever works best, do it often. Whatever will help you bounce back with a vengeance on Monday morning, that is where your time will be best spent.

4. Specific, well-chosen leisure activities

I have a friend who is amazing at Frisbee golf. It is incredible to watch him play. He lives near a course and makes use of it all the time.

I, on the other hand, apparently have absolutely no coordination with my wrist and forearm and would have more success paying someone to play in my place.

If you have a leisure activity that brings you joy, peace, recovery, social time, or just makes you smile—make time for it. You may not have time for it every day, but what if you could make time twice a week?

What if you could guarantee time on your calendar for an activity that truly lights you up? Think about that, then schedule it.

5. Push forward on your career

As I phased out of my marathon-running phase I quickly jumped on the business bandwagon and grew my career, and, years later, this book is a result of that effort.

If you are an aspiring entrepreneur, or have a side hustle in mind, or would love a promotion at the office, using your free time to push your career forward could be the best use of your nights and weekends.

Many people hold down a full-time job and a part-time job at the same time. I did that for years while living in Boston just after college. Think of your off the clock career-building time as a part-time job and you could easily make tremendous progress very quickly.

6. Family time

The most common questions I receive from my podcast listeners revolve around how to handle productivity as a busy parent.

The simple answer, and one that everyone intuitively knows, is that family time will wiggle its way to the top of your priority list whether you want it to or not.

In some seasons of life, family time consumes all of your time—and that is okay. Not only is it okay, but that is also your priority now and attempting to do much else may prove to be too exhausting and counterproductive.

Acknowledge where you are, embrace it, make the most of it, and enjoy it! This season will eventually end, and another will begin.

7. Bucket list

We all have those goals that we have just never made time for, despite our hopes and dreams about where we should have been by now.

If regret drives much of your decision making, fix it. Do something about it.

Spend your free time figuring out how to climb Mt. Everest, learn to speak Portuguese, or get your skydiving license.

Life is short. Your time is now. Stop waiting and starting moving forward.

QUICK REVIEW: *WHAT TO DO WITH ALL THAT FREE TIME*

1. **Free time is not Netflix time.**

   You have endless options when it comes to how you spend your free time. Yes, some of it could be spent on pure entertainment, but changing your default behavior can dramatically improve your results. You can spend your free time progressively working toward results you truly and enthusiastically care about, or you can numb out, disappear, and dissociate with the real power you have over your activities.

2. **Decision fatigue is leading to mindless behavior.**

   When your free time results in reckless behavior or total stagnation, nothing productive is getting done. Mindless free time is wildly ineffective, and you will eventually find yourself engaging in destructive behavior because that is what we do—we take shortcuts, we become reckless, or we just sit on the couch.

3. **You have more free time than you think and you have plenty of options on how to best use the time you have.**

   Considering that free time can either be squandered or seized, the choice is obvious: it is best to choose high-value activities with phenomenal returns on our investment. Mindless free time is out and mindful free time is in.

CHAPTER 10 ACTION PLAN

1. **Brainstorm ideas for all of the possible ways you could optimize your free time.**

   Your free time is your time. You can do whatever you want with it, but it is best to approach it proactively. Make a list of all the ways you would like to spend your free time, focusing on recovery, enhancing your vital few goals, and keeping balance with anything truly important that may be falling behind.

2. **Create structured time off.**

   Just because you have "free time" does not mean you cannot have a clear plan for that time. We often misuse weekends, letting them become two-day lounging sessions instead of rejuvenating, life-producing opportunities. Structure your time off to get the most value out of every day of the week, and every hour of the day.

3. **Set up boundaries to prevent wasting your free time.**

   Sometimes we rest too much, watch too much television, or simply relax to the point of diminishing returns. Setting up boundaries can help you recover properly, and then get back to action before you fall victim to lethargy and stagnation.

STEP

VI

Prevent Future Nonsense

11

Slaying the Distraction Dragons

Death by Distraction

I asked my wife, Tessa, what she thinks about when she thinks about distractions. This was her response:

> My dog, *my spouse*, food, projects, nature, napping, anything online, exercise, stretch breaks, instant messaging, other people, to-do lists, updating to-do lists, adjusting things on my desk, chores, people coming and going, working on projects you don't care about…and all other imaginable things.
>
> —Sanders, 2017

Yeah, that just about covers it—**all imaginable things** can become distractions. There is no limit to what can distract us, or how we can distract ourselves.

In their book *Living Forward*, authors Michael Hyatt and Daniel Harkavy discuss "the drift," a concept that embodies our innate tendency to drive ourselves off course (Hyatt and Harkavy 2016, 28).

We have one intention, but we do something else. We start with a plan, but it quickly dissolves. We want something to be true, but it never materializes. We begin working on something important, only to be distracted again and again... and again and again.

It is death by distraction.

We spend so much time in our lives dreaming about a better future and planning for a better life but rarely do we longingly dream about all of the interruptions that will inevitably stand in our way and throw a wrench in our carefully laid plans.

Distractions are the enemy—they are our nemesis and our greatest foe.

Free time is a wonderful thing, but even in our time off the clock we can distract ourselves from doing what we most desire.

HOW DISTRACTIONS ACTIVELY WORK AGAINST US

1. Distractions increase the time it takes to complete a task.
2. Distractions lower the quality of our work by derailing our creative and innovative minds, which require focus to dig deep.
3. Distractions make us feel frazzled and overly busy.
4. Distractions make us appear out of control and unable to execute a task.
5. Distractions reinforce our desire to procrastinate and postpone hard, yet ultimately meaningful work.
6. Distractions endanger our lives (and our progress) when we take our eyes off the road (and off the target).
7. Distractions make us dopamine seekers—always trying to get the next "hit" instead of aiming for a deeper and richer experience.

Assuming distractions truly are our nemesis, it is baffling to believe that *we are the ones* opening the front door and inviting this evil character right into our living rooms.

We carry distractions around in our pockets and purses as we actively seek to be distracted every time the current moment fails to fully capture and satisfy our ever-shrinking attention spans.

It is human nature to be distracted, to have a million thoughts running through our minds each day, to find it increasingly difficult to sit still or stick with a single task for more than a few minutes.

It takes discipline, deliberate practice, and a strong desire to achieve deep focus to overcome our predisposition to inviting distraction into every known crevasse of our existence.

Fortunately, there are many simple actions we can take to prevent, derail, and forever eliminate the distractions that stand between us and our vital few goals.

STEP VI: PREVENT FUTURE NONSENSE

Up to this point, you have accomplished quite a bit, from completing your self-evaluation and time audits to clarifying your goals and scheduling specific time to bring those goals to life.

The sixth step of *The Free-Time Formula* is to prevent future nonsense—blocking the interruptions that make goal achievement so difficult on so many occasions. This step is divided into two parts: blocking self-imposed distractions and blocking others from distracting you.

Distracting Yourself

1. Deep, Focused Work
2. Slaying the Self-Imposed Distraction Dragon

3. Distracted by Physical Needs
4. Distracted by Your Environment
5. Distracted by Unfinished Work
6. Distracted by Technology
7. Distracted by Your Own Ideas

Distracted by Others

1. Lock the Door
2. Chaos to Clarity
3. When to Say Yes
4. When (and How) to Say No
5. Seventeen Focus Rules

DEEP, FOCUSED WORK

> *I will live the focused life, because it's the best kind there is.*
>
> —Winifred Gallagher (2010, 14)

In your quest to prevent future nonsense, free up time, and block all potential distractions from your vital few goals, one of the core strategies is to repeatedly schedule and achieve deep, focused work.

Deep, focused work is 100 percent distraction-free time with a singular objective.

It is an opportunity to reach levels of creativity and innovation that are simply not possible when you quickly scratch the surface of your work.

Going deep and blocking distractions will improve the quality of your work and provide an incredible sense of achievement when you are finished. It saves time, both now and in the future.

Save Time Now to Save Time Later

One of the core tenets of *The Free-Time Formula* is to spend the least amount of time on any one task, to free up as much time as possible for other tasks.

If you want to maximize your free time for what you care about most (e.g., your vital few goals), your other life activities should take up the least amount of time they possibly can. Efficiency is necessary, and deep, focused work is a highly efficient strategy.

Rory Vaden describes a similar concept in his book, *Procrastinate on Purpose*, in that your goal is to multiply time (Vaden 2015). In other words, spend time today on tasks that will free up dramatically more time in the future.

Deep, focused work is not only a means to improve the quality of your task at hand, but it also acts as a multiplier, freeing up much needed time for other work.

Distractions, on the other hand, are the antithesis of deep work.

Distractions not only prevent you from doing any one thing well, but they also prevent you from doing everything efficiently. Distractions waste time and stand in direct opposition to the deep work that optimizes the few precious hours you have available each day.

Scheduling Deep Work

Cal Newport, author of one the best books on this subject, *Deep Work*, breaks down four philosophies of scheduling deep work, each varying depending on your ideal schedule and desired working lifestyle (Newport 2016).

- **Monastic:** working for weeks or months in a row on a single project
- **Bimodal:** spending multiple focused days on your work
- **Rhythmic:** scheduling smaller recurring blocks of time each day
- **Journalistic:** diving into each priority as it pops up

Focused work can happen whenever it makes sense for you. The key is to determine what is ideal in this season of life, and what is best for the work you are pursuing.

Focus Is a Skill, and It Requires Practice

If you rarely allow yourself the time to dig deep into anything, your first focus sessions will be both incredibly challenging and incredibly rewarding.

Focus is a skill, and you can improve with intentional practice.

The more deep, focused work that lands on your calendar, the more progress you will make and the more encouraged you will be to repeat that process over and over again.

As we are about to discuss, the most important factor in ensuring you get to your focus sessions (and stay there) is creating impenetrable boundaries—barriers to distraction that cannot be crossed by anything.

The firmer your boundaries become, the easier it will be to focus, and the stronger your focus muscles will grow.

This process requires an element of self-discipline, but the hardest part is not ignoring a shiny object that pops up—it is deciding ahead of time which shiny objects are not allowed to distract you and preventing yourself from even catching a glimpse of their allure.

Create Your Focus Checklist

One of the best strategies to enter a focus session prepared is to first run through your focus checklist, a simple list of tasks to complete to ensure you are ready when the timer begins.

Here is an example of my checklist, which I hang on the wall in my office:

1. Get a snack and drink
2. Restroom break
3. Hang up a "Do Not Disturb" sign
4. Turn off phone/tablet/watch
5. Light a candle (just for fun!)
6. Set a timer
7. Turn on website blocking software
8. Turn on focus music
9. Put on headphones
10. Go!

This checklist ensures I have blocked some of my greatest distractions:

1. Hunger/thirst
2. Physiological needs
3. Other people
4. Technology
5. Environmental noises

The key is to preempt what normally causes you to go off on a tangent and stop working, even for a moment.

Brainstorm a list of your greatest distractions that arise when you want to work. Using that list as a guide, create your focus checklist to ensure you can begin your next session as ready as can be.

SLAYING THE SELF-IMPOSED DISTRACTION DRAGON

From the outside looking in, distracting yourself seems silly.

—Really? Can't you just stay focused and get your job done?
—Well, no. It is hard work!

There is an endless number of distractions available to us because we get very creative when we decide not to do something.

I could argue that we are at our best when we are avoiding work because we know just what buttons to push and which tasks to pursue when an important task is looming nearby.

I will break down five common categories of internal, self-imposed distractions and procrastination techniques—the kind of interruptions we voluntary place between ourselves and our goals.

Be warned that this five-headed distraction dragon could grow another head—meaning that this list is far from comprehensive.

As you continue reading this chapter, you may end up creating a brand new category (allowing the dragon to grow a sixth head . . . or a seventh), and discover many more reasons to do anything else besides finishing the book.

As I said, we are amazingly creative when we want something (or strongly desire to *not* do a specific something).

DISTRACTED BY PHYSICAL NEEDS

I have to pee again.

Truly. Today I drank an abundance of water, coffee, and tea as I sat down to write this chapter.

That was a mistake.

Physical distractions like bathroom breaks, a growling stomach, and even feeling antsy because you have not yet exercised today can all be unbelievably distracting.

It baffles me how much time most people spend each day traveling to and from the restroom, or the watercooler, coffee pot, break room, restaurant, kitchen, grocery store, or even the gym.

We commute between doing our work and taking care of our needs, between trying to focus on our work and thinking about refilling our coffee cup again.

We waste an incredible amount of time caring for ourselves when we could be making progress on our goals.

Now, this is not an argument to stop caring for yourself. On the contrary, this is an argument to care for yourself more efficiently, to save time by predicting your normal behavior and tweaking it to dramatically increase your time spent focusing.

Had I planned my day better, I could have minimized my liquid intake, increased my work output, and remained properly hydrated.

A combination of effective planning and keen self-awareness can go a long way toward ensuring you have managed your physiological needs, and yet made enormous strides toward your vital few goals for the day.

On the flip side, I will note that these distractions can work to your advantage in some key ways.

1. Running to the restroom can get you out of your chair and on your feet.
2. A quick trip to the company break room can provide some much-needed social time in the middle of a hard day.
3. Leaving the office for a quick run to Starbucks can spark a new creative idea.

There are pros and cons to managing your physical distractions. What matters most is ensuring you are intentional and savvy about when and how often you balance your true needs with the temptation of yet another obvious procrastination technique.

DISTRACTED BY YOUR ENVIRONMENT

Have you ever started working on an important project and then immediately realized you chose the wrong location to work?

I frequently travel to a local university here in Nashville to write. The campus is beautiful, the library is quiet, and they have phenomenally fast Wi-Fi.

Early on a Sunday morning late last summer, I snuck into their Student Activity Center because the library was closed and this particular building has a great lounge room with plenty of quiet space to work.

My only mistake was timing—it was freshman move-in day.

Within an hour of beginning my work, I was surrounded by families, suitcases, pizza parties, and plenty of awkward glances from people clearly wondering why I was studying when classes had not yet begun for the fall semester.

No, I am not the kind of guy who studies for a class before the syllabus has even been handed out.

When it comes to eliminating distractions, your environment is a deal breaker.

If you choose wisely, you can remain focused and on task for hours on end. If you choose poorly, you can waste an enormous amount of time and end up giving directions to students at a school you don't even attend.

I don't know what it is about me, but I get asked for directions everywhere I go—even in new cities when I am on vacation.

I think it is because I walk fast and appear to know what I am doing.

Though it is true that your environment is not technically a self-imposed distraction because you cannot fully control every aspect of what goes on around you, you do have a lot more power than you think.

The key is to focus on your controllables, the elements of your environment over which you do have power, including the location itself.

When choosing where to work, choose locations with your ideal conditions:

- Predictable temperature
- Easy access to restrooms and restaurants
- Quiet background noise
- Clear of clutter or other visual distractions
- Access to Wi-Fi or other required technology
- Ability to hide in a crowd or block interruptions from others

Once you find an ideal environment, make the most of it. Schedule as many focus sessions as possible in that location and get to work. The more you can accomplish in these sessions, the more free time you will have for other activities.

DISTRACTED BY UNFINISHED WORK

I attended a fun podcasting conference in Chicago a few years ago but ran into a problem right away—I was too busy to enjoy it.

I realized on the first day that I had more going on in my head than I could manage and this was not going to work well if I wanted to network, learn new strategies, and have a great time in the Windy City.

My problem stemmed from the fact that I had booked too many projects before and after the conference.

I gave myself no flexibility, so when it was time to focus on attending a great event, I was mentally absent.

When you attempt to do too much, you cannot do anything well.

When you are trying to focus on an important task, but find yourself continually thinking about all of the other work you have to do, you stress yourself out and delay the work you are so desperate to complete.

I find that this often applies to shallow work as well: email, small and insignificant tasks, anything that should probably get done but that you just do not have time for in the moment.

Unfinished work is an enormous distraction. In *Getting Things Done*, author David Allen refers to this phenomena as open loops, tasks that are not yet complete and require some action to get them done or close the loop.

> *Anything that does not belong where it is, the way it is, is an "open loop," which will be pulling on your attention if it's not appropriately managed.*
> —Allen (2015, 14)

To appropriately manage your unfinished work, it is best to have less work to begin with. What I should have done then, and now do religiously, is cancel, postpone, and reschedule all major projects before and after I travel—or I do not travel.

You will need a solid boundary like this one to clarify what you commit to and what you let go. Getting your work done will certainly clear it from your mind, but so will never letting that work land on your task list in the first place.

When in doubt, purge.

DISTRACTED BY TECHNOLOGY

I am a sucker for social media.

I love it, but it certainly does not return the love. In fact, I am baffled by how much time I spend actively seeking to find something more interesting online than what I am currently doing in the moment, only to be sorely disappointed again and again.

Technology is a tool, nothing more.

Phones, tablets, computers, and other gadgets exist to serve a purpose, to help us get our work accomplished, or to achieve a specific outcome.

Technology, and specifically social media, does not exist to supplement our inability to entertain ourselves or stay focused on the task right in front of us.

Although that may be the intent of those who run social media companies, it is not in our best interest to fall victim to their intelligently designed distraction machines.

How to Best Block Distractions from Technology

1. **Delete your account.**

   Go hardcore right away and just delete your distractions. Any platform that does not significantly enhance your business or personal life needs to go.

2. **Turn it off.**

   As opposed to simply turning the sound off, turn off the device entirely. Remove the ability to be distracted by something that now cannot communicate with you.

3. **Create a focus account.**

   Create a second, stripped-down user account on your computer that cannot access the websites or applications that tempt you away from your work. I used a secondary focus account on my laptop to write this entire book. It works like a charm.

4. Get a website blocker.
Since I often find many websites too tempting to ignore, it is quite helpful to build in a boundary. I highly recommend the Freedom App (https://freedom.to) to block websites on multiple devices at the same time.

5. Turn off all notifications.
Though I have been doing this for years, I often find that most people leave their notifications turned on by default. Nothing is more distracting than another pop-up, ping, ding, ring, badge app icon, banner, or alert that has no business drawing your attention away from what matters most.

6. Schedule time.
Only check Facebook or reply to email if you scheduled time to do so. Creating timed focus sessions specifically for social media, news outlets, or other distracting time wasters can greatly reduce your interruptions.

7. Only use well-built, well-maintained technology.
One of the greatest problems with technology is that it breaks, gets hacked, or just needs to be updated frequently. Avoid the distraction of outdated, slow, and painful-to-use technology by taking care of the tools you choose to use.

DISTRACTED BY YOUR OWN IDEAS

Brains are incredible idea factories.

It is best to think of your brain as a brilliant tool to innovate, dream, and create—as opposed to memorizing endless amounts of data you could find with a quick search online.

When you optimize your brain's ability to think critically and creatively, it will amaze you and produce more and more fascinating results.

However, the biggest drawback to pushing your brain to generate new thoughts is that it will do it, and do it well, and do it often.

Easily, my greatest distractions are my own thoughts.

Whether I am thinking about a new project, a brilliant epiphany that just appeared out of nowhere, or another task that is going to get tackled next, my brain is on the prowl for more stimulation and thought production.

Write It All Down

If you want to eliminate the endless distractions produced by your mind, write down everything you think.

One of the greatest strategies that I lean on every single day is the power of writing down my thoughts, new ideas, and aha moments.

I carry a pen with me at all times, and I have done this for over a decade. Though I now jot down most thoughts straight into my task manager on my phone, I still frequently find myself writing down thoughts with old-school pen and paper every single day.

A helpful strategy to clear your mind through writing is daily journaling, or specifically, using Julia Cameron's "morning pages" strategy from her book *The Artist's Way* (Cameron 2002, 10).

Though it gave me writer's cramp, she advocates waking up each morning to freewrite three pages, "strictly stream-of-consciousness," with pen and paper (no typing).

The goal is to get all of your unrestricted, judgment-free thoughts out of your head and onto paper.

Simply take action by writing down whatever you are thinking about.

It is cathartic, healing, and calming. The more you have on your mind, the more effective this strategy becomes.

Mel Robbins's *5 Second Rule* comes in handy here as well. "*If you have an impulse to act on a goal, you must physically move within 5 seconds or your brain will kill the idea*" (Robbins, 2017).

Writing down your ideas as soon as they arise brings them to life and also provides you with the relief of not trying to remember everything.

QUICK REVIEW: *DISTRACTION DRAGON*

1. **Distractions are the enemy.**

   They are our nemesis and our greatest foe. Distractions increase the time it takes to complete a task, and they lower the quality of our work by derailing our creative and innovative minds, which require focus to dig deep.

2. **Deep, focused work is 100 percent distraction-free time with a singular objective.**

   It is an opportunity to reach levels of creativity and innovation that are simply not possible when you quickly scratch the surface of your work. Both going deep and blocking distractions improve the quality of your work and provide an incredible sensation of achievement when you are finished. Deep work saves time, both now and in the future.

3. **Technology is a tool, nothing more.**

   Phones, tablets, computers, and other gadgets exist to serve a purpose, to help us get our work accomplished, or to achieve a specific outcome. The best method to block distractions from technology is to delete your account. Go hardcore right away and just delete your distractions. Any platform that does not significantly enhance your business or personal life needs to go.

CHAPTER 11 ACTION PLAN

1. Prioritize deep, focused work.
There are only a handful of tasks, goals, and work objectives that make the biggest difference in your results. Deep, focused work is required to bring your A game and execute your vital few projects. When you directly pursue focused work, you give yourself the best chance to increase the quality and quantity of what matters most.

2. Create 100 percent distraction-free work environments and batches of time for your most important daily objectives.
Even the smallest of distractions can throw you off course and derail your productivity. When you eliminate every possible interruption (self-imposed or otherwise), you will find that doing your work is significantly easier, and you will increase the odds of tapping your normally hard-to-find wellsprings of creativity.

3. Acknowledge how you distract yourself most often and make a specific plan to eradicate it.
We all have distracting bad habits, our worst tendencies that pull us out of focus and into another activity besides the only one that matters in the moment. Whatever you tend to do, be honest about it and make a plan to stop it. Barricade yourself. Set up roadblocks. Do what it takes to kill off what is killing your productivity.

12

Turn Off the Lights and Hide!

Lock the Door

Though I have always been a fan of productivity, I became fascinated with strategizing every detail of my life and work when I was hired as the registrar of a college in Nashville.

In one of my many careers in my twenties, I finagled my way into a job that requires immense organizational skills. The registrar of any school is responsible for thousands of tiny details and managing many piles of paperwork, filing systems, student records, schedules, transfer credits, diplomas, and a multitude of other duties.

Within a few weeks of settling into my new position, it was evident I needed more skills, better systems, more efficiency, and most importantly, more space for myself to think and work.

Throughout my day I would receive dozens of phone calls, instant messages, emails, and drop-ins from students, faculty, and staff.

The work I was responsible for was tedious and required a meticulous approach to ensuring every *t* was crossed and every *i* was dotted. I had my own office, but staying focused on any singular task was next to impossible with the endless flood of distractions pouring in at every hour of the day.

I began taking a hard-line approach to my availability.

At first, I put a sign on my door that read "Conference Call" during the key hours that I needed to focus. The sign was a bit of a lie, but it worked like a charm. Most people assumed I was unavailable and came back later, or not at all.

My boss caught on to this trick in a few days, so I frequently changed the wording to "In a Meeting," "Out to Lunch," or simply "Busy. Come Back Later."

I also deleted the instant messaging program from my computer, unplugged my office phone or sent incoming calls straight to voicemail, and turned off my email program as often as possible.

If the need arose, I would also lock my office door, turn off the lights, and work in the filing closet. I would also leave my office and work in the school's adjacent storage warehouse or even in my car.

Whatever it took, I ran, hid, and tried every trick in the book to make myself as hard to find as I could.

Blocking distractions from other people is not only essential to do your best work, but it is also necessary to do any work, regardless of importance.

Other people mean well, they often need your help, and teamwork is a critical component of any highly-functioning home or workspace.

However, that does not mean other people get to dictate your time, availability, or willingness to drop what you are working on to assist them and their "emergencies."

Boundaries!

We need more of them, more often. *Lots more.*

More boundaries, more restrictions, more signs that read "Go Away."

It sounds harsh until you realize the potential—the upside— the beauty in creating magnificently efficient systems that allow everyone to do his or her best work as often as possible.

CHAOS TO CLARITY

Our daily productive output is largely based on our inputs— what we allow into our heads and what we intentionally block. If you want to get more done, defining your communication systems is epically important.

There is an enormous difference between feeling pulled together and running around with your hair on fire. But what does it take to get there? How can we set up working environments that breed predictable rhythms of focus and productivity?

Getting from chaos to clarity, especially in the office, is based primarily on our systems of communication—how much (or how little) we allow others to contact us and interrupt (or work within) our own productive rhythms.

Consider the following four strategies that can help clarify who gets your attention and who does not, when they get your attention and when they do not, which technology is best for getting the job done and which tools are nothing more than endless distractions.

1. Clarify the role of communication in your work

How important is communication for you? Does your normal communication move you closer to your goals, or is most of your communication just busywork or activity?

If your day job is based on your ability to communicate constantly, like a receptionist or call center employee, then your role is clear. If you do just about anything else, communicating that frequently will likely return poor results over time.

Outline how much communication you believe is necessary to get your most important work accomplished and consider how you can limit every other input.

2. Identify your critical partners

One of the easiest ways to clarify who you communicate with, and how often, is based on how important others are to your work objectives. This may be a bit challenging, but categorize those with whom you work into two groups: critical partners and everyone else.

Critical partners are individuals you need to push your own goals forward. They could include business partners, close colleagues, or certain family members. These folks are your productive allies, the ones who will ensure you make tremendous progress. The goal with critical partners is to create win-win communication systems by scheduling your time around each other. Their assistance is vitally important to you, and no one else can fill their shoes.

Every other person outside of this small group of critical partners falls into the second group, people who will get your attention AFTER your primary goals have been achieved. These are people who are not essential in helping you achieve your current goals and, unfortunately, who will have to wait until time on your schedule is freed up. The goal here is to create win-lose communication systems by scheduling time with these individuals in the margins of your calendar.

3. Define your office hours

To help address the reality that you will need time to work with others who are not your critical partners, set aside specific time on your calendar to be available and responsive.

Create office hours where you are physically available to answer questions in person, or use this time to schedule meetings with others for secondary projects. It is also helpful in many situations to create digital office hours where you make yourself available to answer questions via email, chat, social media, Slack, or other systems. You can often get a lot done in a short time period when you batch secondary communication in specific time blocks.

4. Consolidate your communication channels

Of all the strategies I could recommend regarding technology, consolidation is at the very top. We have more tools, channels, and platforms today than ever, which makes it all the more important to use the fewest number you possible can.

Begin with email and forward all of your email addresses to one single account. You may end up with one work address and one personal, which works well. The goal is to avoid having to check eighteen addresses, which will result in missing messages and letting important communication fall through the cracks. For any accounts you do not use and cannot forward, setup auto-replies to let everyone know where you can be found today.

This same strategy applies to social media as well. Post announcements in locations you do not use and tell others where they can find you. For example, if you leave a message for me on my business Facebook page, you will receive an auto-reply to email me at the one email address I actively use.

WHEN TO SAY YES

Rarely.

Saying yes requires something special.

In chapter 4 I discussed *Thirteen Strategies to Filter Your Ideas*. Many of those filters can apply directly when deciding whether or not to agree to a new request or to allow someone space on your calendar.

- Is the new request a 9 or 10? No? Walk away.
- Would the request directly or indirectly generate significant results?
- Would this request qualify as necessary or required to move one of your vital few goals forward?

Be ruthless here.

This is your life, your time, your precious hours on the line.

There are some scenarios where saying yes is not only a great idea, it is the best idea to ensure you can dramatically improve your current circumstances.

1. **When you have no other choice.**

   If your boss mandates it, and you like your job, do it. Much of life falls into the category of obligation—just be sure you clarify what is necessary and what is optional.

2. **When you have nothing planned.**

   Open space on your calendar is an amazing opportunity to be present and open to new experiences. This is great chance to try something new, to connect, learn, grow, and explore a new direction—or to simply schedule something important you have been neglecting.

3. **When something is missing.**

If you feel like there is something missing in your life that could be helped out by joining forces with others and starting something new, dig in. When you find yourself in a rut, and it is clear you need to shake things up, agreeing to a new request could be the turning point you have been looking for.

4. **When it is the first day.**

The first day of a new school year, job, trip, or program is an ideal time to say yes to whatever comes your way. This is your opportunity to become a sponge and see what is available. Once you have your bearings, you can begin the elimination process.

5. **When the offer is too good to pass up.**

Breaking your own rules is part of the game. If an amazing opportunity lands in your lap, and it could change your life in a significant way, strongly consider doing it. Knowing when to say when is highly subjective, but if the offer is a game changer, make it work.

Saying yes is all about direct progress

The shortest distance between any two points is a straight line, and the fastest and most efficient means of getting from where you are to where you want to be is direct, forward motion.

As a general rule, I do not say yes as often as I used to because I found myself drifting in random directions. I said yes to so many opportunities that I pursued too many and succeeded at very few.

If you want to achieve your vital few goals, pursue them to the exclusion of everything else. As Derek Sivers, founder of CD Baby, phrases it, it is a *"HELL YEAH! or No"* (Sivers 2009).

Saying yes is the Ace in your pocket. Use it sparingly.

WHEN (AND HOW) TO SAY NO

My wife, Tessa, has two undergraduate degrees, two master's degrees, and a doctorate in education.

She worked full-time while earning her final two graduate degrees and proved to me beyond a shadow of a doubt that when you want something ambitious, you can make it happen.

In the last semester of her doctoral program, she was working an average of sixty hours every week at her job, taking three classes, and finalizing her 150-page dissertation.

How is this lifestyle possible?

Focus—pursuing an ambitious goal to the exclusion of everything else.

During her tenure as a grad student, she said no to just about every opportunity that popped up. She had clear reasons to turn down others and prioritize her time. She said no over and over again.

Her free time (hours off the clock from her job) was preplanned for studying, researching, and writing. There was little room for anything besides sleep.

The result? She got a lot done, did the important work every day, and ultimately ignored things that could and should have waited until later.

Saying no was hard in the moment and I know she was dying to say yes to many opportunities, but it was clear that the current season needed to end before a new one could begin.

On that note, I did drag her to a farm during the fall for a few hours to play games and run through a corn maze. It was my job to help keep her sanity intact!

When to say no

1. When you have everything planned to the gills
2. When a request does not align with your current highest priority
3. When you are confident about exactly where you are and specifically what must be done
4. When you want to push forward, accelerate your progress, and see real achievement in a specific direction in your life
5. When you feel like there is something necessary that needs your full attention for an extended period of time

Saying no is all about focus

It is time to stop reacting to other people's emergencies.

The inclination to please others, as opposed to directly pursuing your highest ideals, highlights the difference between voluntarily climbing mountains versus inadvertently fighting fires, or proactively doing what matters most on your task list versus reactively acquiescing to the demands of others.

There are only so many hours in the day, and you have so many goals to tackle.

You cannot do it all, and you should not do it all. You cannot say yes to everything, and you should not say yes to most things.

Saying no is not optional, it is merely a question of where you draw the line and how firmly you hold your position.

How to say no

1. No.
2. Sorry, I already have plans.
3. Nope.
4. Wish I could, but that day is already booked.
5. No, maybe next time.

6. After I finish _____, I would be happy to reconsider the offer.
7. No, for real. Stop asking.

The goal is a clear no, said with grace. There is no need to be too harsh unless you truly cannot get the other person to back down.

However you choose to say no, be clear that the answer is no and stick to your guns. Leave no wiggle room for the other person to "get back with you" or "check in a few days later."

Say no and mean it.

SEVENTEEN FOCUS RULES

1. Never answer the phone again.
Unless it is an actual emergency, or you are expecting an important phone call, turn off the ringer and never answer your phone. If the caller truly needs you, you will get a voicemail. You can then return the call at your convenience.

2. Never respond to open-ended text messages.
If you receive texts like, "*What's going on?*" ignore them. Do not respond. If the other person has a real question, your incoming text will ask a question worth responding to.

3. Never get roped into endless group text messages.
Conversations with multiple people are best in person. Group texts, group emails, and most group dialogues lose focus as soon as they begin. Opt out as soon as you have what you need and do not reengage without good reason.

4. Never stop what you are doing for someone else's bogus emergency.
This is worth repeating. It is your time, not theirs. It is your priority, not theirs. If others fall behind and need your help

to get caught up, they will wait until it is convenient for you. Soon they will realize you are not the one to call when they wait until the last minute.

5. **Never argue with anyone online.**
   There is enough nonsense on the Internet to fill a thousand lifetimes—do not contribute to the noise. Not only does it waste your time, but you also are not changing someone else's opinion, and you are not serving a higher purpose through irate Twitter rants. Arguing online is a total waste.

6. **Never answer emails when you are angry.**
   I am guilty of this on more than one occasion. If you are not sure if you should hit send—you should wait. Give it a day or two, come back to the email, and then decide. I will often write an email in Evernote, save it, and then copy it into my email program if the message is truly worth sending.

7. **Never sleep with your phone turned on, or in the same room as you.**
   Years ago, I began turning off my phone at night and charging it in my office, not my bedroom. Allowing your phone to wake you from sleep, or to be at your bedside when you first wake up is a great way to begin your day distracted. Just turn it off.

8. **Never attend meetings.**
   It is hard to imagine a bigger waste of time than most meetings. If you want to reclaim your calendar, start here. Drop out of committees, tell your boss you have something more important to work on, and cancel any recurring meeting that does not directly push you toward your goals.

9. **Never attend meetings without a clear end time.**
   For the few meetings you must attend, clarify when they will end and end them on time. The more ruthless you are with

ending your meetings, the more likely you are to prevent additional wasted time for inefficiencies that popped up during the meeting itself.

10. Never have coffee with strangers.

I get asked to coffee quite a bit. I love coffee and great conversations, but the vast majority of coffee dates will not significantly enhance your life. Choose wisely when saying yes to a "quick coffee." They are rarely quick and, without a clear agenda established upfront, can easily become burdens to your already overbooked schedule.

11. Never attend an event without a clear exit strategy.

I once attended a three-day conference for less than three hours. I realized the conference was not the highest and best use of my time, so I left and did not return. That weekend I accomplished tremendously more than I had planned and proved that every event needs a way out. If you find yourself attending events you should not be attending, walk out the door.

12. Never work for a micromanager.

Have you ever tried focusing with someone standing directly behind you and watching your every move? I used to have a boss who would not only stand over me but would correct every tiny detail of my work in the moment and afterward. Distractions at this level will destroy any ability you have to do your best work. If you can, get out of that scenario. If you must, change jobs.

13. Never design your office for constant collaboration.

There are specific locations that are best for collaboration, but your day-to-day workspace is not one of them. Top performers produce mediocre work when collaboration is a priority in the office because they (and you) need to focus. The goal is to optimize your office for focus and producing amazing results, and to be intentional about when and how everyone works together.

14. Never read a book word for word.

There are few books that need to be read word for word. To save time and pick up the most benefit from your reading material, plan to skim for highlights and avoid reading anything cover to cover. This one strategy can save you dozens of hours per month and allow you to read more than ever.

15. Never endlessly scroll through social media apps.

Social media is fun, entertaining, and fluffy, but not suited for deep, meaningful work. Deactivate or delete your social media accounts that do not serve a great purpose in your life. If any platform is utterly distracting and proves not to be helpful, let it go.

16. Never make it easy to check social media.

Go ahead and remove all social media icons from the home screen of your phone. Also, remove distracting apps from the desktop and dock of your computer. Any technology that encourages you to quickly check in to see what others are up to will result in checking in way more often than is necessary.

17. Never continue doing something you would not do again.

When in doubt, let go of everything and start with a clean slate. If you were not currently committed to it, would you seek it out again? If you would not rejoin a group, restart a relationship, or apply again for your current job, it could be a sign it is time to walk away from all of it.

QUICK REVIEW: *TURN OFF THE LIGHTS AND HIDE!*

1. We need more boundaries.

Blocking distractions from other people is not only essential to do your best work, but it is also necessary to do any work, regardless of importance. Other people do not get to dictate your time, availability, or willingness to drop what you are working on to assist them with their "emergencies."

2. Saying no is all about focus.

There are only so many hours in the day, and so many goals to tackle. You cannot do it all, and you should not do it all. You cannot say yes to everything, and you should not say yes to most things. Saying no is not optional, it is merely a question of where you draw the line and how firmly you hold your position.

3. Never answer the phone again.

There are so many habits we acquire over time based on good intentions or old systems that used to be effective. In our world today, distractions come from every direction at all times, and we have to draw a line somewhere.

CHAPTER 12 ACTION PLAN

1. Say no by default.

From now on the answer is no. The only way you will be able to maintain your sanity long term, and get anything done, is to change your default response to no for any new request. This simple change will free up more time than most other strategies available to you, regardless of what you do now or plan to do in the future. The answer is always no.

2. **Lock the door.**

   Make the decision now to kill off your external distractions. Turn off your phone, lock your office door, turn off your overhead lights, and hide from your coworkers. Do whatever it takes to ensure no one else can distract you when you need to focus. Never let them beyond the barrier. You are in control of your time.

3. **Get your whole team on board.**

   Nothing works better than teamwork when everyone is on the same page. To make your distraction barriers as strong as possible, persuade your boss, coworkers, and team members to adopt these same strategies. When everyone focuses on priorities, it is incredible how much more can be accomplished in a very short amount of time.

VII

Solidify Your Ideal Rhythm

13

Crunch and Release

When Pushing Hard Pushes Back

What I am about to share with you is tough, but it is an important message that I could not leave out of the book.

I had a tough season after my trip to the emergency room. It was a season filled with more stress, anxiety, and work than I had ever experienced.

In the heart of this season, I hit a wall. I had just finished a podcast interview that I thought went very poorly.

I ended the interview with a clear sense of frustration, angst, and regret. I also knew I needed to get my feelings out of my head as a cathartic means of calming down and figuring out exactly what to do next.

I hopped onto Facebook and just started typing.

What I ended up writing truly surprised me. It was more real and open than I had ever been on a public platform.

These were feelings I had in my head, but rarely spoke aloud or shared with others—even my wife.

It was not a marketing ploy, as some perceived, but rather a public venting session to help keep me from a near certain breakdown.

I hesitated before I hit the post button.

I was legitimately scared to share some of my darker moments, not only with strangers online but especially with my close family and friends who knew nothing about what I was experiencing in private.

I am sharing this with you now for the same reason I shared it at the time, which is to make one point very clear: *you are not alone.*

- Whatever it is you are fighting, *you are not alone.*
- Whatever your struggle, *you are not alone.*
- Whatever your biggest obstacles in life are today, *you are not alone.*
- Whatever your grandest ambitious happen to be, *you are not alone.*
- Whatever you are hiding from, you are not alone, and you do not have to fight your battles in private.

Here is the unedited post in full.

Facebook Post: August 17th at 5:58 pm

Moment of truth here.

I'm a productivity guy, but you know that already.

I'm ambitious.

I'm driven.

Yes, and yes.

I'm also edgy, hostile, and sometimes too angry for my own good.

Surprised?

In the last 9 months, I have filed more BBB complaints against companies I work with than ever before.

I ended up in the ER in May for a stress-related condition.

I have panic attacks.

I don't sleep much and I drink too much caffeine.

I work 80–100 hours a week by choice.

I don't have a stop button.

Sometimes I'm a mess, and it's hard to see any of that online. You can't actually, because I don't talk about it.

I have a nice headshot and a pretty website, but I'm more of a real guy than you realize when looking only from the outside.

Yes, I have a few good ideas and I share any brilliance I come across to help others—but mostly, this journey began as a cathartic practice of self-healing.

I began blogging in 2009 to figure out what I wanted out of life. That evolved into me desperately trying to answer tough questions by pushing harder.

I ran a dozen marathons, wrote a few books, and pushed harder.

I have always leaned on pushing harder—using blunt force to solve any problem.

It's not healthy, and I know it.

I'm working on it, but it's a journey that doesn't have a clear ending yet.

In the meantime, know this: I am struggling too.

I have my own demons to battle and my own obstacles to overcome. I need to talk about this stuff more.

I really do.

So, if you see any outbursts from me online, you'll now have some context as to where the passion is coming from.

I want the best for myself and others.

I have a high bar of excellence and most people fall short of it all the time.

It's not their fault—it's my bar.

I also fall short of my bar all the time. Maybe it's time to take it down a notch?

Maybe.

Probably.

Until then, I'll keep trying to find what works and I'll share the journey.

Thanks for being a part of this and for supporting me.

I am forever grateful.

STEP VII: SOLIDIFY YOUR IDEAL RHYTHM

To summarize what we have covered so far, let's run through a hypothetical scenario where you have effectively completed each step of the formula.

Imagine you completed *The Free-Time Formula Self-Evaluation* and *Time Audits*. By asking the right questions and determining exactly how your time is being spent, you now have a greater sense of where you are today and what is getting done.

You then clarified your *vital few goals* that will make the greatest impact on your future success. After reviewing the *Five Stages of Project Prioritization* and *Thirteen Strategies to Filter Your Ideas*, you were able to efficiently organize your goals and determine what the next best steps should be.

You then prioritized a quick but intense daily exercise session of *interval training*, followed closely by a few minutes of *mental bicep curls* (meditation). By flexing your physical and mental muscles, you were able to sharpen your ability to move forward with increased clarity, energy, and enthusiasm.

After reviewing your calendar, you determined it was more than necessary to *cut the nonsense*. There were many tasks to eliminate, material possessions to donate, and commitments to opt out of forever. You effectively *reduced the ongoing friction* that was holding you back from making direct progress on your vital few goals.

You then designed your own *Red-Carpet Calendar*, complete with your highest priorities scheduled first, and plenty of focused *batching sessions* on your customized *theme days*. After reviewing the *Three Planning Models of Free Time*, you mindfully chose the best activities in the margins of your calendar to help you replenish your energy and get back to your craft every day.

Finally, you identified exactly how you are consistently distracting yourself and intentionally set up barriers to keep you on track. Also, due to the ongoing interruptions from your coworkers, you set up clear external boundaries to help others recognize when you need a little space to do your most creative work.

194 The Free-Time Formula

This brings us to the seventh and final step of *The Free-Time Formula,* which is to solidify your ideal rhythm, and it is divided into two parts: crunch and release, and your seven-day action plan (see chapter 14).

Ideal Rhythms

1. Crunch and Release
2. Work Hard, Play Hard

Seven-Day Action Plan

1. The Value of One Action Step
2. Seven-Day Action Plan
3. Final Message
4. #FreeTimeFormula
5. Resources

CRUNCH AND RELEASE

There is an ideal rhythm to work and play that unleashes your best self.

Author and speaker Todd Henry puts it this way, *"Hustle brings incremental results, rhythm brings intuitive leaps"* (Henry, 2017).

For reasons that are hard for me to articulate, I have always intentionally hustled and worked hard for what I want, but I cannot say I have always intentionally prioritized a rhythmic approach to achieve intuitive leaps.

Hustle gets results, but it is short-lived. Hustle is the drive that pushes you to finish the marathon or the big project at work, but how will you have the energy, enthusiasm, and creativity for the next marathon or the next big project?

Rhythm is the crunch and release that creates the opportunity for infinite intuitive leaps.

Digging in to work hard is what pushes you forward. Immediately following this productive session could be a well-deserved, well-designed, and purposeful recovery period—the kind of recovery period that replenishes you and allows for continual progress long into the future.

Rhythm allows for sustainability. It creates a routine that allows you to repeatedly access your greatest creativity and your best self over and over again.

The story I shared to open this chapter is a pristine example of hustle run amok. Rhythm was totally absent from my calendar. Taking a break was a fantasy and pausing to purposefully recover would have felt like a clear waste of time.

That approach failed miserably.

Hustle is a small piece of a larger puzzle, a puzzle dominated by purposeful recovery, crunching and releasing, working hard and playing hard.

WORK HARD, PLAY HARD

Peter Awad, host of *The Slow Hustle Podcast,* is a shining example of a man with a well-balanced plan.

As an entrepreneur and father of four children, you might expect his life to be continually chaotic or holistically unsustainable. His reality, however, is much more rhythmic, balanced, and beautiful.

For much of the year, Peter, his wife, and all four kids travel together in a motor home around the United States. Working remotely, Peter can grow his business on the road while maintaining a close connection to his family and seeing more of the world every year than many do in a lifetime.

Peter works hard to keep his business running, and he plays hard by prioritizing his family time and his desire to stay mobile as often as he can afford to do so (Awad, 2016).

RHYTHMIC SABBATICALS

Systematically taking time away from your work on a regular basis is paramount to your ability to stay fully engaged when you are working, and totally unplugged when you are not.

Sabbaticals are traditionally designed for academics to break from their normal teaching schedule to travel, study, and research, often for many months at a time. For our purposes, think of a sabbatical as precious time away from your normal routine to replenish your soul and reengage with your greatest passions.

Consider when, and for how long, you could guarantee quality time for recurring sabbaticals in your current season of life and work:

Daily: How could you guarantee an hour or more for "me time"?

Weekly: When is it best to take a step back to pause, reflect, and regroup? Could you guarantee a work-free zone for one to two days each week?

Monthly/Quarterly: How can you free up a few days each month for bigger picture planning, or intentionally getting away for a quick trip?

Semi-Annually/Annually: Have you preplanned an extended vacation or retreat to fully decompress from your normally busy schedule?

Working hard and playing hard are two sides of the same coin. We need to work hard to provide for ourselves and our loved ones, but we also need to play hard for the same reasons. There is more to life than work, and there is an ideal rhythm to life that can sustain your soul. Crafting that lifestyle is a bit of a challenging art form, but it is a challenge worth accepting.

QUICK REVIEW: CRUNCH AND RELEASE

1. **Pushing hard can push back.**
   When you are in a tough season, it is immensely beneficial to get your feelings out of your head as a cathartic means of calming down and figuring out exactly what to do next. Remember that *you are not alone*. Whatever it is you are fighting, *you are not alone*. Whatever your struggle, *you are not alone*.

2. **Hustle brings incremental results; rhythm brings intuitive leaps.**
   Hustle gets results, but it is short-lived. Rhythm is the crunch and release that creates the opportunity for infinite intuitive leaps. Rhythm allows for sustainability. It creates a routine that allows you to repeatedly access your greatest creativity and your best self over and over again.

3. **Working hard and playing hard are two sides of the same coin.**
   We need to work hard to provide for ourselves and our loved ones, but we also need to play hard for the same reasons. There is more to life than work, and there is an ideal rhythm to life that can sustain your soul. Crafting that lifestyle is a bit of a challenging art form, but it is a challenge worth accepting.

CHAPTER 13 ACTION PLAN

1. Pull back.

Learn from others who have pushed too far. Pull back before you fall off the cliff. It is all too common to get overly ambitious and pursue new goals at a rapid and unsustainable pace, only to find yourself crashing and burning. If you find yourself getting frazzled, pause to regroup, make a new plan, pull back, and then only push forward again when you are truly ready.

2. Solidify your ideal rhythm.

We all have our own unique rhythms that allow us to live our best lives. Your rhythm will look different from mine, and each of our rhythms will fluctuate from one season to the next. Take a little time between goals, or between seasons, to identify what your next season could look like if everything were ideal. Use this template as a guide to living your best life.

3. Commit to working hard, stopping, and then playing hard.

There is a time to celebrate, though you have to stop working to do so. If you are like me, working is the norm, and pausing to "play hard" is tough. Make the call to balance time spent on your craft with legitimate leisure activities. When you look back at your life a year from now, you will smile at those moments. Taking time off is part of your productive flow, so be sure to enjoy yourself!

14

Seven-Day Action Plan

The Value of One Action Step

There is incredible value in taking direct action.

In fact, the smallest and seemingly most insignificant actions are inherently more valuable than the eighteen new things you learned but did nothing about.

In your quest to acquire more free time, achieve your most important goals, and live a more prosperous life, the only strategy that ultimately matters is the one that creates the results you want—and, ideally, in the shortest amount of time possible.

Every other strategy you could adopt is, therefore, not as valuable and deserves little or none of your attention.

A single action that pushes you directly toward your goal builds momentum. It gets the ball rolling and knocks down the wall of inertia standing between you and what you want most.

As a productivity coach, I have worked with many high achievers who fall victim to the same traps as the rest of us.

One of the most common traps is valuing activity over productivity, busyness over progress, and nonsense over results.

We come to believe that if we stay busy enough, surely *something* important is getting done, right?

Unfortunately, no. Being busy only leads to being busier.

In the process of valuing activity over productivity, you will accomplish some important tasks, but at a huge cost: increased stress, fatigue, burnout...you know the drill.

Your mission in everything you do is to identify the single action that is the very next most important task to accomplish. That single action will have more value than a dozen indirect actions that keep you feeling busy, but ultimately going nowhere.

Put some deep thought into the actions you take, the events you attend, the projects you take on, and the goals you decide to pursue with an enthusiastic fervor.

Every action matters.

Every single one.

SEVEN-DAY ACTION PLAN

Now that you have reached the end of the book, it is time to bring *The Free-Time Formula* to life. I encourage you to follow this simple plan over the next seven days.

Take one direct action per day.

Move closer to your goal of acquiring more free time, more balance, more achievement, or simply more rest.

1. Complete the Self-Evaluation and Time Audit.

On day one, the best first step is to find out what's going on in this season of your life. The Self-Evaluation and Time Audit should take no more than an hour to complete unless you want to dig in deep on the evaluation questions.

2. **Clarify your vital few goals for this season.**

   Depending on where you are in your current season, this will either be incredibly obvious or quite challenging with a complex web of tasks to wade though. Either way, write down the select few goals that matter the most right now—goals that you will be building your life around for the next few months. The fewer goals you commit to, the easier every other step in the process will be.

3. **Solidify a plan to exercise for ten minutes each day.**

   Choose a simple but effective exercise that will get your blood pumping. Interval training and strength training are two effective possibilities, but be sure to check with your doctor and personal trainer for a customized health plan.

4. **Scan your calendar and cut every bit of nonsense you possibly can.**

   This is a fun day! Cutting nonsense is a highly rewarding activity. Take your time here and cut everything you can. Be willing to make some difficult decisions.

5. **Schedule a focused batching session for one vital goal.**

   I recommend scheduling a two- to three-hour block where you can completely focus on one task. If you normally do not have focused blocks like this, one session can change your life forever.

6. **Identify your greatest distraction and make a plan to eradicate it forever.**

   Start with one, and then next week you can tackle another. Some distractions are sneaky and will resurface easily.

Plan accordingly and fight your nemesis with everything you've got!

7. **Create a firm boundary to stop work for the week and enjoy yourself!**
   There is work time, and there is play time. When the whistle blows, stop. When the free time shows up, take advantage of it. Purposeful recovery is a powerful tool to replenish what you need and begin again next week.

FINAL MESSAGE

As a final parting message, I hope that reading this book has served you as much as writing it has served me.

I opened the book with a peek into the darker side of productivity, how prioritizing achievement over wellness lead me to the dire consequence of landing in the emergency room.

I want to end the book on a hopeful note because that is what I feel today: hope.

Productivity is a dirty word for many people because they believe it represents just doing more things they do not want to do. In my world, productivity has always been a grand and hopeful opportunity to accomplish unbelievable goals and truly bring dreams to life.

I am sure that, like me, you want more—more achievement, more prosperity, and more free time to enjoy the best parts of truly being alive.

Along the way, take a moment to pause.

Take some time out of your busy schedule to look around, ask some tough questions, regroup, and begin again more intelligently.

Getting the results we want and truly living a life of prosperity happens when we do the few things that make the biggest difference. If we do not pause now and then, we will likely find ourselves back in the storm of activity, missing the simple and profound moments of stillness.

This is a journey. Unfortunately, there is not a magical end destination that will provide all the answers to the questions posed in this book.

However, there is something beautiful in the mystery and uncertainty that comes from being human.

I hope you achieve your own happiness, focus, and productivity in the midst of your mystery, and that the ideas in this book can help you structure a direct plan to achieve what matters most to you.

QUICK REVIEW: SEVEN-DAY ACTION PLAN

1. **Every action matters.**
   The smallest and seemingly most insignificant actions are inherently more valuable than the eighteen new things you learned but did nothing about. Your mission in everything you do is to identify the single action that is the very next most important task to accomplish. That single action will have more value than a dozen indirect actions that keep you feeling busy, but ultimately going nowhere.

2. **Take the next seven days to jump-start your free-time plan.**
   There are many actions you can choose from, so start in the beginning and progress one step at a time. The Seven-Day Action Plan provides the starting blocks you need to bring your *Free-Time Formula* to life.

3. **Take a moment to pause.**
   Take some time out of your busy schedule to look around, ask some tough questions, regroup, and begin again more

intelligently. Getting the results you want and truly living a life of prosperity happens when we do the few things that make the biggest difference.

#FREETIMEFORMULA

Be sure to use #FreeTimeFormula when you tell all your friends online about how much nonsense you just cleared from your calendar.

If you want to connect with me directly, you can explore my website, JeffSanders.com, find me on Twitter, @JeffSandersTV, and on Facebook, JeffSanders.com/facebook, and even send me an email, Jeff@JeffSanders.com.

RESOURCES

1. **Free Bonuses!**
   Readers of *The Free-Time Formula* get free access to a variety of bonus materials to supplement the book including a guided workbook, book club questions, templates, and more. Sign up: www.JeffSanders.com/FreeTimeBonus.

2. **The *5 AM Miracle* Podcast**
   The 5 AM Miracle is dedicated to dominating your day before breakfast. Learn the latest self-improvement strategies and dive deep into everything from healthy habits and early mornings, to personal development and rockin' productivity. Listen to the podcast: www.5amMiraclePodcast.com.

3. **The Rockin' Productivity Academy**
   Designed for high achievers and entrepreneurs, *The Rockin' Productivity Academy* provides ongoing community, support, monthly training videos, and exclusive interviews with

successful people from a variety of industries. Learn more: www.RockinProductivity.com.

4. **47 Strategies: A Productivity Self-Assessment**
   If you are looking for a way to boost your productivity, this is a great place to start. The *47 Strategies Self-Assessment* analyzes your current level of productivity and then offers up advanced strategies to optimize your ability to get more done every day. Learn more: www.47Strategies.com.

5. **Additional Recommended Reading**
   Now that you have finished this book, here are a few phenomenal reads that will optimize your productivity and success.

- *Living Forward* by Michael Hyatt and Daniel Harkavy
- *Deep Work* by Cal Newport
- *The 5 Second Rule* by Mel Robbins
- *The More of Less* by Joshua Becker
- *The 5 Choices* by Kory Kogon
- *The Obstacle Is the Way* by Ryan Holiday
- *Finish* by Jon Acuff
- *10% Happier* by Dan Harris

References

Allen, David. *Getting Things Done* (revised ed.). New York: Penguin, 2015.

Awad, Peter. "The Power of a Slow Hustle with Peter Awad." Jeff Sanders. Published October 10, 2016. Accessed August 20, 2017. https://www.jeffsanders.com/the-power-of-a-slow-hustle-with-peter-awad-podcast-172/.

Becker, Joshua. *The More of Less*. Colorado Springs: Waterbrook Press, 2016.

BusinessDictionary, s.v. "Parkinson's Law." Accessed July 29, 2017. http://www.businessdictionary.com/definition/Parkinson-s-Law.html.

Cameron, Julia. *The Artist's Way* (10th anniversary ed.). New York: Tarcher/Putnam, 2002.

Covey, Stephen. *The 7 Habits of Highly Effective People* (25th anniversary ed.). New York: Simon & Schuster, 2013.

Fagan, Sean. "Which Disney Princess Are You?" *BuzzFeed*. Published February 3, 2014. Accessed September 17, 2017. https://www.buzzfeed.com/mccarricksean/which-disney-princes-are-you?.

Gallagher, Winifred. *Rapt*. New York: Penguin Press, 2010.

Hardy, Darren. "Secrets of Great Achievers." Published July 3, 2016. Accessed August 23, 2017. https://www.youtube.com/watch?v=pefcqT0bjM4&feature=youtube.

Harris, Dan. *10% Happier*. New York: HarperCollins, 2014.

Henry, Todd. "Why Your Constant Hustle Is Getting You Nowhere." Todd Henry. Published June 14, 2017. Accessed August 28, 2017. http://www.toddhenry.com/productivity/constant-hustling-getting-nowhere/.

Hof, Wim. "The Beginning of the Iceman." Iceman Wim Hof. Accessed September 3, 2017. http://www.icemanwimhof.com/wim-hof-iceman.

Hyatt, Michael, and Daniel Harkavy. *Living Forward*. Grand Rapids: Baker Books, 2016.

Matthews, Michael. *Bigger, Leaner, Stronger* (2nd ed.). Des Moines, IA: Waterbury Productions, 2015.

Matthews, Michael. *Thinner, Leaner, Stronger* (2nd ed.). Clearwater, FL: Oculus, 2015.

McKeown, Greg. *Essentialism*. New York: Crown Business, 2014.

Millburn, Joshua Fields, and Ryan Nicodemus. "What Is Minimalism?" *The Minimalists*. Accessed August 29, 2017. http://www.theminimalists.com/minimalism/.

Newport, Cal. *Deep Work*. New York: Grand Central Publishing, 2016.

Onstad, Katrina. *The Weekend Effect*. San Francisco: HarperOne, 2017.

Onstad, Katrina. "You're Doing Your Weekend Wrong." *QZ*. Published June 23, 2017. Accessed August 14, 2017. https://qz.com/1012585/the-best-weekend-activities-are-most-likely-not-the-ones-youre-currently-doing/.

Robbins, Mel. "The 5 Second Rule." Mel Robbins. Published April 2, 2016. Accessed August 3, 2017. https://melrobbins.com/the-5-second-rule/.

Ryce, Ted. "Fitness for Busy People with Ted Ryce." Jeff Sanders. Published December 28, 2015. Accessed August 15, 2017. https://www.jeffsanders.com/fitness-for-busy-people-with-ted-ryce-podcast-131/.

Sanders, Tessa. Discussion with the author. August 2017.

Sivers, Derek. "No 'Yes.' Either 'HELL YEAH!' or 'No.'" Sivers. Published August 26, 2009. Accessed August 12, 2017. https://sivers.org/hellyeah.

Tierney, John. "Do You Suffer From Decision Fatigue?" *New York Times*. August 17, 2011. http://www.nytimes.com/2011/08/21/magazine/do-you-suffer-from-decision-fatigue.html.

Vaden, Rory. *Procrastinate on Purpose*. New York: TarcherPerigee, 2015.

Whelan, Cory. "What Is an Esophageal Spasm and How Is It Treated?" *Healthline*. Published July 27, 2017. Accessed September 24, 2017. https://www.healthline.com/health/esophageal-spasm#overview1.

About the Author

 Jeff Sanders is the author of the popular productivity book *The 5 AM Miracle* (2015), and he is on a mission to help you dominate your day. Through his popular podcast, also called *The 5 AM Miracle*, Jeff speaks on how to bounce out of bed with enthusiasm, form powerful lifelong habits, and tackle your grandest goals with extraordinary energy.

Jeff is a keynote speaker, productivity coach, personal development fanatic, and plant-based marathon runner. He has a bachelor of arts degree in Theatre and Psychology from Truman State University and lives in Nashville, Tennessee, with his lovely wife, Tessa, and quirky pug, Benny.

To learn more about Jeff and his current projects, visit JeffSanders.com.

Index